Where is the

The Mystery of the
Marquette & Bessemer No. 2
Second Edition

by
Thomas Adams

Pack Ice Press - Cleveland, OH
2024

ISBN: 9798218493509
Library of Congress Control Number: 2024913656
Cover photo courtesy of the Father Edward J. Dowling,
S.J. Marine Historical Collection of the
University of Detroit Mercy Library.

Acknowledgements

I dedicate this book to the many people who have helped me or paved the way for me to tell this story. The first three I wish to mention are deceased prior to my starting this project, and whom I have never actually had the pleasure of meeting.

Donna Rodebaugh: Donna Rodebaugh was niece to both Robert and John McLeod. Her father, H.D. McLeod, was planning to replace John McLeod as first mate on the *Marquette & Bessemer No. 2* at a future date, but this never happened as the ship was lost. (*Ashtabula Star Beacon*)[i] Donna Rodebaugh spent many years compiling information about the wreck and even mounting expeditions to explore possible leads as to the vessel's location. Her passion in trying to solve this mystery appeared to be relentless.

Robert William Jones: Mr. Jones, I am told, was from Sarnia, Ontario. I am told Mr. Jones is deceased, but that he is largely responsible for collecting and donating much of the hard copy material about the *Marquette and Bessemer No. 2* that now resides in the Historical Collection of the Great Lakes at Bowling Green State University Library. Without his efforts, it is unlikely that a book of this depth on this type of subject would have been possible.

Dwight Boyer: Mr. Boyer lived in the Cleveland area and passed away in 1978. He was a newspaper reporter for the *Toledo Blade* from 1944 to 1954 and the *Cleveland Plain Dealer* from 1954 to 1978. Had he not translated his passion into books about the Great Lakes, I would not be writing this volume today.

Carolyn McVean Adams: She was my mother who was good enough to keep me in book money as the occasion arose. She would likely be surprised I wrote a book, though I think she would have enjoyed this one.

Louis N. Adams: He was my father, and he would have simply skipped ahead to the last chapter to see how it ends.

David J. Adams: He is my brother and a professional writer and poet. Without his assistance, this book would not have been possible.

Additional thanks go to the following,

Mark Peter Spang: The archivist at the Historical Collection of the Great Lakes, Bowling Green State University. Mark has been both tolerant and helpful as this novice writer has wandered and sometimes stumbled through the research process. His assistance, support and patience have been invaluable and much appreciated.

Patricia Higo: The archivist at the Father Edward J. Dowling, S.J. Marine Historical Collection of the University of Detroit Mercy Library who has procured for me some wonderful photos for this book. She was always gracious when I needed "just one more picture."

Christine Renko: She has delivered both copious amounts of coffee, and no small amount of sass required to keep this project going, as well as critical technical assistance in preparing this book for publication. She was the layout designer for this book.

John Koch: John's logic and significant firsthand knowledge of diving and Lake Erie shipwrecks has been an invaluable resource. If only I could give you a legitimate target on the American side.

Alan Flaherty: Alan was gracious enough to be my technical editor regarding nautical detail on this project.

Gina Dewaele: Assitant Archivist of the Elgin County Archives for helping me with great photos and information.

Cindy Prather: Assistant Director of the Conneaut Public Library, who was a great resource with local material and helped with navigating older issues of the Conneaut News-Herald.

Contents

Introduction

"Still a good distance away, the glass of Captain Jerry Driscoll discovered the forms of several men sitting in the bottom of the little boat. He saw that their faces were red. By appearance, they were alive, but they sat very still, with their heads hanging low and their eyes closed. 'They're exhausted,' said Captain Driscoll.

As the Perry drew within hailing distance the crew shouted to the men in the boat, but received no answer. The boat rode as evenly as before over the low waves, the heads of its silent crew did not move, and no answer came. 'They're dead said Captain Driscoll.' "[ii]

—*The Cleveland Plain Dealer*, December 13th, 1909.

Most people enjoy a good mystery, or even better, a good ghost story. I wonder if that is as true today as when I was growing up in the 70's. In our era of instant information, communication and technology, a mystery is a rarer commodity unless it is part of an Internet clickbait story. It is hard to believe that an era prior to cable TV and the Internet was only a relatively short time ago. Reading was much more prevalent, and kids who wanted a mystery read Sherlock Holmes or the Three Investigators stories. My mind today wanders to the Oak Island treasure hunt series on the History Channel that was originally spawned by a *Reader's Digest* story that appeared in the 1960's.

In my case, I always thought more about the mysteries and ghost stories of shipwrecks in the Great Lakes. While my parents weren't always people of ample means, my mother always found enough cash to make sure I was well stocked with books, many of which I still own. Books were expensive then, so this was no small accomplishment. My fascination with Great Lakes shipwrecks began with her buying me a copy of Dwight Boyer's 1968 volume titled *Ghost Ships of the Great Lakes*. This volume was one of several books about the Great Lakes written by Boyer, a longtime newspaper reporter. Boyer's book covered major shipwrecks from all over the Great Lakes, including a chapter dedicated to the railroad car ferry *Marquette & Bessemer No. 2*. The ship was often called just "No. 2." When Boyer's book was published, the majority, if not all, of the ships discussed in it had sailed off into oblivion, never to be heard from again. The majority of those wrecks have since been found, but not the No. 2, and that story was one the most

1

compelling.

I think part of the attraction was that I live right on Lake Erie and the unresolved story of the No. 2 has struck close to home. Another facet that drives my interest is the myriad of confusing and contradictory clues the story presents. Then there is the fact the No. 2 was lost in the shallowest of the Great Lakes, yet it eludes detection to this day. It is one thing for a ship to vanish in the depths of Superior in 1909, but Erie? The story of the No. 2 is a story about a shipwreck, but also one with a haunting feel to it. While I did not realize it when I started writing this book, the sinking of No. 2 also represented a convergence of the turbulent changes going on in 1909. To my twelve-year-old self, it was a local mystery filled with unknowns and a little terror. It is also a story that takes us back to a profoundly different time than the one we live in today.

On Tuesday Dec. 7th, 1909, the *Marquette & Bessemer No. 2* left the port of Conneaut, Ohio and sailed into what would become a brutal December storm that took 59 lives, destroyed 4 ships and one tow barge. (*Duluth Evening Herald*)[iii] To this day, the No. 2 has never been found, remaining stubbornly hidden in the relatively shallow depths of Lake Erie. Part of the mystery is the great uncertainty as to where and exactly when she sank, with various clues supporting some highly divergent theories. With improved technology and advanced techniques, these Great Lakes mysteries are falling by the wayside. The discovery of the S.S. *Hydrus* in Lake Huron in 2015 marks the discovery of the last ship missing from the Great Storm of 1913. Each year brings us at least partial answers to the fates missing ships and their brave crews. As these fantastic time capsules into our past will slowly degrade with time, even in the favorable cold fresh water of the Great Lakes, their discovery becomes even more important. The risks from zebra mussels and souvenir hunters are omnipresent.

As I moved deeper into this story, the flood of clues became more difficult to assess. They are sometimes contradictory. I have also learned that newspaper and eyewitness reports of the day may or may not be accurate. In many cases, a report or a clue must be viewed within the lens of probability. In other words, how likely are these reports or clues to be true or accurate. A following question then emerges. Can the clue be partially true or simply the most accurate recollection at the time?

Regardless, we are still left with the central questions. Where is the *Marquette & Bessemer No. 2*? What can the wreck tell us? How much different was the world of that crew than the world we live in today?

Many bright people through both video and the written word have contributed to narrowing down the possibilities, but the fate of the ship and her crew still eludes us. I believe she will be found soon. As technologies improve, and with the pending survey by NOAA of much of the lake, her hiding place may be revealed. My endeavor with this book is to review the story and take a closer look at the clues. Perhaps we can narrow the hunt. The crew deserves the final chapter of their story to be told. Part of me will be elated when the No. 2 is found, and a small part of me will be saddened as another mystery falls by the wayside.

Note

In this volume I cite from many sources, some of which are more than a centurey old. Particularly in newspaper sources, the conventions of typography were widely varied, and often different from those of the current time. Please note that such sources appear here in their original form, including even variations in spelling.

Chapter One: Back to 1909

One must use a little imagination to understand the time and place in which the railroad car ferries operated in in 1909. In the not-so-distant past, vast amounts of product and raw material were transported by sea and by rail. In the 1800's, schooners and barks were the tractor trailers of their era. These ships supplied towns and cities and stimulated commerce all over the Great Lakes and were crucial to the economic development of the region. By 1910, steel ships had rapidly replaced wooden sailing ships and steamers, which were becoming an increasingly rare sight. (Toledo Blade)[iv]

As lake ships evolved into steel hulled steamships, the dynamic hadn't changed much except that they became larger and more efficient. The Interstate system didn't yet exist, and marine and rail transport were king. The railroad car ferries represent a hybrid marriage of sorts of the two modes of transport. These ships, which plied the lakes from the late 1880's to the 1960's, were employed to solve logistical problems of the railroads. Some lines, like those surrounding Lake Michigan, served to avoid the log jam of rail transport in large cities like Chicago, where trains could disappear for days on sidings in overcrowded rail yards. Sometimes, smaller car ferries were used to navigate rivers where bridges were not yet present. (Babbish)[v]

In the case of the No. 2, the ship facilitated the movement of rail cars north from Western Pennsylvania to Canada. These railroad cars primarily carried coal or other raw materials. Every day, the *Marquette and Bessemer No. 2* would make the five-hour run north from Conneaut, Ohio to Port Stanley, Ontario with a cargo of roughly 30 loaded rail cars on her car deck. One of the economic challenges of this is that this flow of cargo was often one way, with the ship often returning to Conneaut with only a cargo of empty rail cars. Still, it was cheaper and faster than running a train longways around Lake Erie to Canada and it was a faster process then that employed by the *Marquette & Bessemer No. 1* which ran coal from Conneaut, Ohio to Erieau, Ontario.

The No. 1 was an unusual design. "Built by the Buffalo Dry Dock Company, the ship had two parallel tracks on her deck, running over strongly reinforced hatches. She loaded from a car ferry slip simply by having the hoppers run aboard her. These cars were unloaded by dropping coal into the hold. At Erieau, the hatches were removed, including the railroad rails, and the coal was removed with a clamshell.

The Marquette & Bessemer No. 1 was smaller than the No. 2 and had a much lower profile. It was a design that was not replicated because of the development of the self-unloader." (Hilton)[vi] She was derisively nicknamed the grasshopper, and Hilton commented that the ship was "anything but a beauty." The No. 1 was renamed the Carrolton in 1936. Regardless, she went on to a very long career as a bulk carrier until she was scrapped in 1961. (Historical Collection of the Great Lakes)[vii] She was captained by Murdock Rowan, cousin to Captain McLeod.

The *Marquette & Bessemer No. 1* was such an unusual ship, and because it takes part in our story, I have included a few photos of it here. Note the open summertime upper pilot house similar to the Marquette & Bessemer No. 2. That is mostly where the similarities end. Photo courtesy of The Father Edward J. Dowling, S.J. Marine Historical Collection of the University of Detroit Mercy. Library.

The split aft cabin on the *Marquette & Bessemer No. 1* allows decking with rails to be put down and railcars and be pulled right onto the deck for unloading. Note how much lower the cargo rides in this vessel compared to the No. 2.

Below is a shot of the deck of the No. 1.

Both photos courtesy of The Father Edward J. Dowling, S.J. Marine Historical Collection of the University Detroit Mercy Library.

Great Lakes shipping in 1909 was nothing like today. The No. 2, like most commercial ships of her day, had no wireless. Radar was decades away. Weather on the Great Lakes can be fantastically volatile, especially late in the shipping season. Sudden and brutal storms capable of tremendous destruction were common. Weather forecasting was an imperfect art. Unlike those on the oceans, Great Lakes vessels did not have the maneuvering room to sometimes avoid bad weather. Wave patterns are shorter, more violent, and ultimately more destructive. Safety and lifesaving equipment were primitive by today's standards. The reality is that steamships on the Great Lakes may only be a few miles from shore, but they were so isolated in bad weather that they may as well have been on the moon. It was on the brink of such a storm that the No. 2 was preparing to leave the Port of Conneaut on Tuesday December 7, 1909.

Railroad car ferries often operated in bad weather. They were typically the first ships out in the spring and some of the last to cease operations as the winter season fell upon the lakes. They were sturdy, robust ships known for their ice breaking ability. Like all lakers, they operated in a period where there was enormous economic pressure to sail. Each trip and each cargo were considered critical for both the ship's profitability and for the reputation of the ship, captain, officers, and crew. It was not unusual for car ferries to sail well into December or January, even after the ship's certificate of insurance expired for the year. However, the "Marquette & Bessemer Dock and Navigation Company did not run their car ferries or the No. 1 year-round and they were laid up for the winter months, usually from the beginning of January to March or April. Regardless, they frequently had to break ice early and late in the season, and, like all Great Lakes vessels, were forced to contend with severe storms." (Hilton)[viii] On the next page are two pictures of the No. 2's crew contending with ice either early or late in the season.

1909 was a particularly challenging and volatile shipping season yet, it was a very successful season for cargo volume. Some ports had record-breaking years for cargo, including a record-setting year for grain shipments at Canadian ports. Many ports throughout the lake handled record-breaking cargo. Two headlines summarize the situation well.

"Over 65,000 trains would be needed to transport freight handled in Duluth-Superior Harbor in 1909." (*Duluth Evening Herald*)[ix] and "Ore Shipments for the Year Beat All Former Records-Over Forty Million Tons Brought from the Upper Lakes." (*Conneaut News-Herald*)[x]

The crew of the No. 2 using dynamite to blast pack ice from the ship. Year unknown. Photo courtesy of the Historical Collection of the Great Lakes, Bowl ing Green State University.

"Just put your back into it." Freeing the No. 2. Note the good view of one of her lifeboats from below. Year unknown. Photo courtesy of the Historical Collection of the Great Lakes, Bowling Green State University.

1909 was also a year with significant shipping losses. Thirty ships were reported destroyed before the December storm in this story took the *Richardson, Henry Steinbrenner, Wissahickon,* and *Ashtabula. (The Detroit Free Press)*[xi] The *Steinbrenner* was sunk in a collision on the Detroit River on December 06,[th] 1909 and raised and rebuilt the following year. She would sink again in 1953 on Lake Superior with a loss of 17 lives. (Historical Collection of the Great Lakes)[xii]

8

The *W.C. Richardson* was wrecked off Buffalo and the *Ashtabula* grounded and flooded in the same storm that destroyed the *Marquette and Bessemer No. 2*. The *Wissahickon* ran aground in this storm and could not be pulled off until January. (*Duluth Evening Herald*)[xiii] It is unclear if the *Clarion*, which burned with a large loss of life, or the *Marquette & Bessemer No. 2* were included in this grim tally. The cost of lives, ships, and cargo in 1909 was a large one.

Early reports have five crew of the *W.C. Richardson* lost, and 14 saved, but later reports would increase that number to 8 lost and 11 saved. Five went down with the ship and three were missing and presumed dead after leaving the ship in a yawl (the ship's small work boat). Among the missing was second mate Sydney Smith. He and two others left the *Richardson* in a yawl seven miles from where she was broken up on Waverly Shoal. (*Duluth Evening Herald*)[xiv] Further, one survivor of the *W.C. Richardson* which sank off Buffalo was even reported to have been made insane by exposure and committed suicide. (*Duluth Evening Herald*)[xv] Of comparable horror, one of the Richardson's lost crew was found frozen solid in a block of ice upon the break wall, "with arms and legs extended, the body was in a position of swimming, trying to reach shore." He was Sidney Smith, only 19 years old, and one of the three men who attempted to leave the *W.C. Richardson* in a yawl. In one report, he is listed as the second mate of the *W.C. Richardson* and seems too young to hold that position. Axes had to be used to free the body from the ice. Among the lost was Mrs. John Brantford, second cook of Cleveland. She appears to be the only women lost in the storm and her body was never recovered. (*Detroit Free Press*)[xvi] Fifteen crewmen were lost in the burning of the *Clarion*. Fourteen crewmen were reported saved from the *W.C. Richardson* and six from the *Clarion*. (*Duluth Evening Herald*)[xvii]

Great heroism and selflessness made the losses less than they could have been. After the *Clarion* ran aground and caught fire, her captain and forward crew were "lost after launching a boat in attempt to reach the lightship Kewaunee, marking the shoal. All were lost. Despite the fire raging below him, the *Clarion's* chief engineer clung to the smokestack ladder, operating the ships whistle by hand, sounding a continuous distress signal. Guided by the frantic whistle sounds, the grain laden steamer, *Leonard C. Hanna*, in a magnificent feat of seamanship on the part of her master, plucked the after crew from the wreck (a return trip was made to save the engineer)." (Boyer)[xviii]

In another feat of extraordinary bravery, 14 crew members of the *W.C. Richardson* were rescued by the steamer *William A. Paine*. (Historical Collection of the Great Lakes)[xix] The *Paine* stayed with the stricken *W.C. Richardson* for thirty hours and was so badly damaged itself that it had to be towed into port. (*The Cleveland Plain Dealer*)[xx]

It was also at the end of this season that the Lake Carriers Association entertained the idea that the shipping season should end December 1st Increasingly, crewmen were reluctant to sail late in the season. Typically, ship's insurance certificates expired on December 5th each year. (*Duluth Evening Herald*)[xxi] Still many ships were out on the lakes handling end of season cargo, some operating under insurance extensions.

In addition to 1909 being both a financially successful and dangerous shipping season, there was also significant labor strife. There were accusations of union-busting leveled at the Lake Carriers Association and reports that some crew members and officers were underqualified for their roles. (*Duluth Labor World*)[xxii] The sources of these problems were complex and multi-faceted. Change evolving over the prior couple decades was culminating in transformation and tension.

"Hard economic times of the 1890's forced consolidation of shipping and other companies into larger, more data-driven entities. Larger steel ships required many more different job classes than traditional sailing ships. Great Lakes shipping, as in other industrial sectors, faced a growing tide of worker unrest at the turn of the twentieth century. Efforts to unionize increased, but three strikes between 1901 and 1908 actually deepened divisions between unions and categories of sailors and weakened the effort as a whole." (Daley)[xxiii]

I do not wish to delve too deeply into the complex labor environment of 1909 but do want to set the stage for the concept that there was a lot of turmoil. "In an effort to provide an alternative path to unionization, the Lake Carriers Association created the Welfare Plan. This plan created rooms in ports with amenities and served as an alternative to a traditional union hall. Officers and crew were encouraged to participate in and hire from the hall, and to disavow unionism." (Daley)[xxiv] The strikes of fragmented unions in 1909 resulted in violence at times and threats of sabotage. The strike unofficially went on until 1912, The Lake Carriers Association declared victory in its 1909 Annual Report, and that the successful drive for an open shop principle had demonstrated its necessity going forward.

At the start of the 1909 strike the International Sailors Union had counted 25,000 members in the US and Canada. In 1910, it fell to 16,000, with most of the losses coming from the Great Lakes." (Daley)[xxv]

Marine Review recorded a startling surge for 1909 and 1910 in strandings, groundings, and collisions compared to previous years. Collisions leapt from 59 in 1908 to 125 in 1909." (Daley)[xxvi] Violence featured heavily in the strike: assaults, robberies, and brawls along picket lines began. Strikers threw stones at boats crewed by strike-breakers. Among the most violent encounters came in Detroit on 19 July as the chief engineer of a non-union ship shot two union men who were threatening him. His claim of self-defense was accepted, and he was exonerated. (Daley)[xxvii]

1909 was clearly a year of dynamic and volatile change. It was a year that saw great financial success, but also terrible loss. It seems clear in looking at the statistical changes, the labor situation impacted safety on the Great Lakes. It also seems clear the Welfare Plan did not provide ships all the qualified crewman they needed.

In February of 1910, inspectors would give a blistering report on the *W.C. Richardson* loss. Captain Burke's license was revoked, and Chief Mate Robinson was suspended for one year. Among the findings were that the "captain lost his reckoning off Conneaut when the cargo shifted. In an attempt to straighten the boat up, ballast tanks were ordered opened and the injudicious use of ballast caused the boat to founder off the Buffalo breakwater after drifting two days in a submerged condition. Further, the ship was reported to be fully manned when it was in fact undermanned and carried a dangerous cargo of flax. The report indicates the crew was very inexperienced, with the majority having been in their first season on the lakes. Several were teenagers, and many were not sailors at all. It is reported the crew had no experience launching or manning a lifeboat. The article further goes on to assign blame to the Welfare Plan policy, which is implied to be a scab union hall supplying the lake boats with unqualified crewmen. (*Duluth Labor World*)[xxviii] While this is clearly a publication with some bias, the carnage of 1909 speaks for itself. The *W.C. Richardson* clearly appeared to be undermanned and crewed by a very inexperienced group.

The following example is telling as to the extent some ships may have been undermanned. Regardless of the veracity of the charges, it is clear this was in the forefront of issues in 1909.

W.C. Richardson on the St. Clair River in 1905. Photo courtesy of the
Richard J. Wright Collection, Historical Collection of the Great Lakes,
Bowling Green State University.

One extraordinary article serves to highlight this issue of adequate staffing.

"Buffalo, March 12th, The United States District Court grand jury returned indictments against the Lake Carriers Association and Albert Limerick, shipping master of the association at this port, charging them with 'shanghaiing.' The indictments cover the cases [of] Albert Stoneberg and John Bovison, boys of about 16 years of age. This is the second time the cases have been presented to a United States grand jury, the first time being at Elmira last fall and the grand jury returned a no-bill against Limerick and the Association. United States district attorney John Lord O'Brien submitted evidence to the present grand jury and had no trouble securing an indictment. 'I propose to put an end to this manning of these immense boats that sail the Great Lakes with inefficient crews and green hands, as was the case many times last summer.'" (*Toledo Blade*)[xxix]

The outcome of this case was unclear based on the information available. What is clear is that in some ports staffing Great Lakes ships with crews that were both competent and of sufficient number was an issue in 1909.[i] *Duluth Evening Herald*)[xxx] The fact this story appeared in a major midwestern newspaper, is, by itself, quite extraordinary.

This was the environment at the end of the 1909 shipping season. Fortunately for the *Marquette & Bessemer No. 2*, the crew and officers had been mostly stable and well-trained. They were fortunate to have a very experienced engineer and a captain widely regarded as one of the best navigators on the Great Lakes. First Mate John McLeod, older brother of the captain, was a very experienced sailor who held his own captain's license as well. As it was a ship that returned to its home port regularly, it was an attractive assignment for experienced crew and officers. Clearly, some of the crew was inexperienced, and some had misgivings about the stability of the vessel after serving on it. While there was some flex and uncertainty with the last couple roster spots on the crew and it appears to have sailed a few hands short on December 7th, it appears they were in an above average situation compared to many of the boats on the lake. Nonetheless, tragedy awaited the No. 2.

On the morning of December 7th, we find the *Marquette and Bessemer No. 2* moored at the harbor in Conneaut, Ohio. The ship had just been loaded with 30 rail cars, 26 of which contained coal totaling 981 tons. Three cars contained 51 tons of structural steel, and one car was loaded with iron castings. (*Erie Times-News*)[xxxi] Regular provisions had been loaded for her round trip to Port Stanley, Ontario. The cars were locked into place on the car deck.

The rail dock at Conneaut Harbor. Photo is undated. Courtesy of the Historical Collection of the Great Lakes, Bowling Green State University.

The *Marquette & Bessemer No. 1* had left port on time at approximately 8:00 AM. She would survive the savage storm coming without incident, though it was a harrowing passage. The departure of the No. 2 was delayed. The previous day, the No. 2 had already endured a very difficult crossing on its return trip from Port Stanley, with Captain McLeod commenting that was one of the worst crossings he had ever experienced. (*Lake Erie Beacon*)[xxxii] Strong winds were already mounting, and a freighter that was laid up for the winter in the harbor had broken free from its mooring, blocking the channel.

This blockage delayed the departure of the No. 2 while captain and crew waited for a tugboat to reposition the wayward ship and clear the channel. Just as the No. 2 was pulling away from its dock, a man came running up to the ship. This gentleman was Albert Weis, a passenger who had business dealings in Canada. Captain McLeod gently backed the ship up so Mr. Weis could jump on. He had just made the ship. Arriving as he did, he would have been a couple hours late. How Mr. Weis knew the ship had not yet left harbor is not clear. "Mr. Weis was the treasurer of both the Keystone Fish Company and the Bay State Iron Works, and one of the best-known businessmen in the city." (*Grand Rapids Press*)[xxxiii] It has been long rumored that he was carrying a large amount of cash to purchase a business in Canada. (Boyer)[xxxiv] In various sources, I have seen the amount speculated between 32,000 and 50,000 dollars, and as far as I can tell, the existence of the money at all is speculation. Undoubtedly, for some wreck divers, this is part of the allure of finding the ship. Based on the amount of wreckage found drifting in the lake, most of the upper structures of the boat were probably destroyed, and after a century under the lake, the money, if it did exist, is undoubtedly unrecoverable.

Weis probably felt quite fortunate to have just caught the ship leaving the dock. He would undoubtedly feel much differently in a few hours as the No. 2 steamed out into the lake to vanish into history. By just making the dock, Mr. Albert Weis's fate was sealed.

Despite the mounting winds, it could not be foreseen that the car ferry would be sailing out into a Lake Erie storm that would destroy 4 ships and take at least 59 lives. The *Marquette & Bessemer No. 2* sailed out into Lake Erie, and shortly, would never definitively be seen again.

Chapter 2: The Ship

The *Marquette & Bessemer No. 2* was a railroad car ferry engaged in the singular purpose of shipping railroad cars across Lake Erie. The ship would occasionally take passengers as well. Most often, that cargo consisted of rail cars filled with coal. In the late 1800's to the end of the Marquette & Bessemer line in 1932, in Canada, Western Pennsylvania coal was used for everything from heating homes to fueling railroad locomotives. Car ferry routes throughout the Great Lakes served a myriad of purposes. They served as a short cut to avoid the log jams of large urban railyards like Chicago, where apparently a train could be delayed for days. In other areas, they might serve as a de facto rail bridge, carrying railroad cars shorter distances across rivers where bridges may not yet be built. (Babbish)[xxxv] In Lake Erie it appears the mission was coal, and taking a train on a five-hour trip across the lake must have been a cost reduction over circumventing the lake. As both Babbish and Hilton pointed out, the flow of coal north was robust, but little cargo was handled on the return trip other than empty rail cars. Passenger traffic was also apparently light. As such, the car ferry traffic in Lake Erie dissipated with the decline of coal as a primary energy source, especially as fuel for locomotives. The last Lake Erie line ended in 1958. (Babbish)[xxxvi]

The *Marquette & Bessemer No. 2* was built in 1905 by the American Ship Building Company. Depending on the source, reports of ship's length vary from 350 or 338 feet with a beam of 54 feet. The ship was to draw no more than 14 feet in the water fully loaded. A fully loaded ship constituted 30 rail cars and 200 tons of coal. Twin triple expansion engines were to provide a speed of 12 mph. (Historical Collection of the Great Lakes)[xxxvii] Her car deck had 4 rails on it.

The *Marquette and Bessemer No. 2* had been ordered by the Marquette & Bessemer Dock & Navigation Company to replace the ill-fated *Shenango I*. The *Shenango I* was built in 1895 and handled the railroad car ferry duties until 1904. The *Shenango I* was of wooden construction and was built by the Craig Shipbuilding Company in Toledo, Ohio. The *Shenango I* was 56 feet shorter than the No. 2. It has been reported that this vessel was underpowered, and therefore left much to be desired as an icebreaker. This may have contributed to the vessel's downfall. The *Shenango I* became trapped in pack ice at Conneaut Harbor during the winter of 1904 and was unable to free itself. (Babbish)[xxxviii] "Captain John McLeod (brother of Captain Robert McLeod and later First Mate of the No. 2) was able to work her back to to the inside of the Conneaut break wall but could get her no further." (Hilton)[xxxix]

The No. 2 in this undated photo. Photo courtesy of the Historical Collections of the Great Lakes, Bowling Green State University.

After being trapped in the ice and biding her time until spring, the *Shenango I* caught fire on March 11, 1904. The fire could not be controlled, and the ship was a total loss. One crewman, Fireman Charles McCarter, was killed, and Chief Engineer Morrell was badly burned in an effort to save him. (Hilton)[xl]

The two photos that follow show the *Shenango I* hopelessly ablaze and corroborate that the ship was a complete loss.

The Shenango I on Fire at Conneaut, Ohio. 1904.

The *Shenango I* on Fire at Conneaut, Ohio—a Second View. 1904.

Both photos courtesy of The Father Edward J. Dowling, S.J. Marine Historical Collection of the University of Detroit Mercy Library.

Very few photographs of the first *Marquette & Bessemer No. 2* exist, likely in part because of the ship's very short service life of only 4 years (1905-1909). Adding to the confusion, the Marquette & Bessemer Dock and Navigation Company ordered a nearly identical replacement car ferry right after the No. 2 was lost. The replacement ship was ready for launch during the 1910 season. Virtually indistinguishable from the first car ferry, the two main physical differences between the original No. 2 and her 1910 replacement were the presence of a stern gate, and the original No. 2 had an open upper pilot house whereas the replacement had a closed one. One other critical difference is the replacement ship had wireless radio. Ten days after the loss of the No. 2, the Marquette & Bessemer Navigation company determined that henceforth, all their ships would be equipped with wireless radio. (*Erie-Times-News*)[xli] Note that this was a company decision and not regulated by the government or embraced by all companies. When the S.S. *Milwaukee* was lost in 1929, even at that late date, the ship had not been equipped with wireless radio, which may have saved lives. It was also very odd that the Marquette & Bessemer Dock and Navigation Company gave the replacement the exact same name, also calling it the *Marquette & Bessemer No. 2*. This was customary for car ferries but led to a great deal of confusion over the years, especially with regard to two ships that are virtually identical that ran the exact same shipping route and had the exact same name.

Following is the most recent inspection of the ship, listing only 2 lifeboats. I am fairly certain this listing is in error. Every account I have seen includes four. Early photos of the ship appear to have only two lifeboats, but all the later photos of the ship have four. Draw your own conclusions here. The minimum crew for this vessel is listed as 25 officers and crew, but it should be noted they ran two shifts on this ship, so some men were usually off duty.

On the following pages are the certificate of inspection and data sheet for the *Marquette & Bessemer No. 2*.

CERTIFICATE OF INSPECTION
FOR FREIGHT, TOWING, AND OTHER STEAMERS OF OVER 100 GROSS TONS

State of *Ohio*   District of *Cleveland*   *Freight* Steamer *Marquette & Bessemer No. 2*

APPLICATION having been made in writing to the undersigned, Inspectors for this District, to inspect the *Freight* Steamer *Marquette & Bessemer* of *Erie*, in the State of *Pa.*, whereof *A. R. McLeod* is master, said Inspectors, having performed that duty in accordance with the requirements of Title LII, Revised Statutes, and the Rules and Regulations of the Board of Supervising Inspectors, on the *5th* day of *October*, 19*08*, DO CERTIFY that the said vessel was built at *Cleveland*, in the State of *Ohio* in the year *1905*; that the Hull is constructed of *Steel*, and, as shown by official records, is of *2574* gross tons; that the said vessel is provided with *1 Triple Exp* Condensing Engine of *19-31-52* inches diameter of cylinder, and *3* feet stroke of piston, and *4* Boilers *12* feet in length and *165* inches in diameter, made of *Steel*, in the year *1905*, and are allowed a steam pressure of *175* pounds to the square inch, and no more. The said vessel is required to carry the following complement of officers and crew: *1* Master, *1* Mate, *2* Mates, *2* Engineers, *4* Firemen and *16* Deck Crew, and is permitted to navigate for one year the waters of the *Great Lakes* *between Erie & other ports*, touching at intermediate ports, a distance of about _____ miles and return.

WE FURTHER CERTIFY that the said vessel at the date hereof is, in all things, in conformity with the law.

THE FOLLOWING PARTICULARS OF INSPECTION ARE ENUMERATED, VIZ:

Load-line draft	___ feet ___ inches	Boiler plate—thickness of	1.25"	Safety valves ... No. 4
Has signal lights	Yes	size 8½ x 9½	Tensile strength of	60,000	Steam gauges ... No. 4
Boats 1 No.	2	Ductility of	26-3%	Gauge cocks ... No. 12
Every lifeboat has equipment in accordance with the rules	yes	Record in local inspectors' office at Cleveland, O		Low-water gauges ... No. 4
Life-preservers No.	1027	Boiler shell ... drilled		Fusible plugs ... No. 12
Double-acting hand pumps ... No.	one	Thickness of plate found	rey inch.	Auxiliary boilers—No. — when built, 1
Hose—Internal diameter	1½ inches	Longitudinal seams	Triple riveted	Where built —
Length of fire hose, feet	581	Heads Drilled		By whom built —
Water buckets No.	25	Steam pressure allowed lbs.	175	Diameter of —
Water barrels No.	2	Hydrostatic pressure applied lbs.	263	Thickness of plate —
Axes No.	2	Flues No.	12	Tensile strength of plate —
Boilers—No.	4 when built, 1905	Length		Record in local inspectors' office at —
Where built Cleveland 1905		Diameter	9' 4½"	
By whom built Amer. Ship Bldg Co		Thickness	.591"	Scheme

State of *Ohio*   County of *Cuyahoga*   ss: *W. B. Nelson*, Inspector of Hulls.   *James McGrath*, Inspector of Boilers.

Subscribed and sworn to before me this _____ day of _____, 190___, by _____, Inspector of Hulls, and by _____, Inspector of Boilers.

Custom-House, _____, 190___.

I HEREBY CERTIFY that the above Certificate is a true copy of the original on file in this Office.

_____ of Customs.

Two copies of this Certificate must be framed, under glass, and placed in conspicuous places in the vessel where they will be most likely to be observed by passengers and others. (Section 4432, Revised Statutes.)

APPROVED MARCH 28, 1906.

V. H. Metcalf, Secretary of Commerce and Labor.

Geo. Uhler, Supervising Inspector-General.

The certificate of inspection of the *Marquette & Bessemer No. 2.* Courtesy of the Historical Collection of the Great Lakes, Bowling Green State University.

UNIVERSITY OF DETROIT
Marine Historical Collection

RECORD OF GREAT LAKES SHIPS

Name MARQUETTE & BESSEMER No. 2 Registry Number US 202314

Year of Build 1905, Place CLEVELAND O.

Name of Shipbuilders AMERICAN S. B. CO Hull Number 428

Dimensions; 338, x 54, x 19.5 : Tons; Gross 2514, Net 1484

Type of Vessel CAR FERRY Built of STEEL

Engines (TWIN) TRIPLE EXP., 19, 31, 52 Dia. x 36 Stroke

Built by A. S. B. CO. Year 1905

Owners of Ship: MARQUETTE & BESSEMER DOCK & NAV. CO.

Changes in Ship's Name: (NONE)

Disposition: FOUNDERED, L. ERIE, 12-7/9-'09, 32/36 LIVES.

Remarks

ALBUM II-6 NEG. See SPECIAL FILE

Record of Great Lakes Ships, Courtesy of the Father Edward J. Dowling, S.J. Marine Historical Collection of the University of Detroit Mercy Library.

Above you can see the blow up of the cover photo of this book showing the open upper pilot house that is a hallmark of the first car ferry. Photo courtesy of the Father Edward J. Dowling, S.J. Marine Historical Collection of the University of Detroit Mercy Library.

The Original *Marquette & Bessemer No. 2* at Port Stanley in 1905. Photo Courtesy of the Historical Collection of the Great Lakes, Bowling Green State University Library.

As I stated earlier, photos of the original *Marquette & Bessemer No. 2* are quite rare. This one is at Port Stanley in 1905. It is one I have never seen before that I am fairly certain has never been published. There does appear to be a single light house. Note how narrow the channel appears to be. Entrance in the conditions presented on the night of December 7th probably would have been impossible without wrecking the ship, presuming the light was fully functional. In this earlier photo, the lifeboats are amidships. This location must have been changed at some point. The forward wall of the upper pilot house is up. This was not always the case in the photos I have seen. The wall must have been detachable and taken down as the summer season wound down.

Unlike its namesake, the second *Marquette & Bessemer No. 2* went on to a long career as a railcar ferry. "After the Marquette & Bessemer Dock and Navigation Company went out of business in 1937, she was sold to Herman Pirchner and used as a "showboat" for the Great Lakes Exposition in Cleveland. Then in 1942, she was sold to the Filler Fiber Company of Manistee and was reduced to a barge to transport pulp wood. She was renamed the *Lillian* in 1946." (Babbish)[xlii]

The No. 2 was very similar to other railroad car ferry designs of the time made by the American Ship Building company, such as the *Pere Marquette No 18* and *Pere Marquette No. 19*. The *Pere Marquette 19* was actually used to cover the route of the No. 2 until the replacement ship was ready.

The *Pere Marquette No. 18* was another ill-fated boat that sank in 1910 in Lake Michigan after mysteriously taking on water. Twenty-seven crew perished, including all her officers. Thirty-five crew and passengers were saved. The wreck of *Pere Marquette No.18* was discovered in 2020 in 500 feet of water some distance off Sheboygan, WI. The wreck is in poor condition, jutting up from the bottom with the stern buried in mud. The decks have collapsed. It has been speculated that leaking was caused by a failure of the hull plates that resulted in her sinking. It had been reported that there was a history of collision during docking that may have contributed to this problem. As the stern is completely buried in mud at a depth of 500 ft. in Lake Michigan, the true cause of her loss will likely never be confirmed.

Pere Marquette No 18. Photo courtesy of the Father Edward J. Dowling, S.J. Marine Historical Collection of the University of Detroit Mercy Library.

As a class of vessels, the railroad car ferries of the time were regarded as sturdy, durable ships capable of ice breaking and staying out much later in the shipping season, as well as being some of the first ships out in the spring. In truth, "the overall safety record of the car ferries is superb. When W.L. Mercereau, marine superintendent of the Pere Marquette railroad, went to Manitowoc in 1926 to supervise efforts to take one of his ferries, *Pere Maquette No.18(II)* off the beach where she had grounded, a reporter thought he had seemed rather unconcerned about the accident and asked him about its severity. Mercereau replied that the affair was routine. Since his ships put into Lake Michigan Harbors 3000 times per year, he was surprised that groundings and harbor collisions were as few as they are." (Hilton)[xliii]

One could argue that the car ferries had a better safety record than other types of vessels, given the number of trips they undertook and the fact they operated in all types of weather. They were not invincible however, as the loss of two relatively new vessels within just a couple years of each other indicates. The *Pere Marquette No.18* was built in 1902 and the *Marquette & Bessemer No. 2* was built in 1905. It is interesting that some of these ships had a very short service life, while others of virtually the same design sailed on for decades without problems. Following is one of the few detailed photographs of the original *Marquette and Bessemer No. 2.*

The original *Marquette & Bessemer No. 2.* Photo courtesy of the Father Edward J. Dowling, S.J. Marine Historical Collection of the University of Detroit Mercy Library.

The previous photo offers great detail about the ship, much of which is relevant to the story of her loss. Notice the additional rear facing pilot house for docking. Three of the 4 lifeboat stations can be seen on this vessel. Note they are forward and midship on the forward superstructure. The ship has 2 spars and two smokestacks. The absence of a stern gate to keep following seas out would come to be considered one of the ship's fatal flaws and may have been a contributing factor in the ship's loss. A stern gate could be lowered to protect the rear of the ship from water coming over the car deck, but also be easily raised to allow loading and unloading of the rail cars.

The theory behind sailing without a stern gate is that in rough weather, one must keep the ship sailing with the bow directed into the waves. The practice apparently was more difficult to execute than the theory would suggest. Following seas could still overwhelm and flood the car deck from the exposed stern. Captain Robert Mcleod, the ship's very experienced captain, had one such harrowing experience during a trip in a November storm, the month prior to the ship's loss. "Captain Mcleod confided to his brother Hugh, he had kept his vesselheaded directly into the waves and when the stern sank down into the troughs between them, the water rushed in, filling her so rapidly that on one occasion the No. 2 had listed so badly that her upper rails were underwater." (Boyer)[xliv] Captain Mcleod had serious doubts that he would be able to save his ship, but was able to recover. "After this episode, he complained quite bitterly, and the Marquette & Bessemer Dock and Navigation Company promised to install a stern gate at the end of the season." (Boyer)[xlv] The storm of December 7th would spare the Marquette & Bessemer Dock and Navigation company this expense. Such was the pressure to sail and deliver cargo in 1909.

One can go back to the photo on the previous page to view the open stern. Subsequent photos are of the museum ship S.S. *City of Milwaukee* located in Manistee Michigan. This vessel, built in 1931, is the only surviving example of early railroad car ferry construction I am aware of that exists intact today. Built by the Manitowoc Shipbuilding Company for the Grand Trunk Railroad, her displacement and dimensions are very similar to the *Marquette & Bessemer No. 2*. Length, beam, and capacity are all very similar. Coming out of service in 1981, she also has a very similar profile to the No. 2. She has the same two stack, two spar configuration. The superstructure and pilot house design are very similar. Cargo capacity (rail cars) is reported to be 30 to 32 cars. We are fortunate such an example still exists. The S.S.City *of Milwaukee* is a more modern ship. She had wireless radio, improved safety equipment, and, critically, a stern gate.

We can see how much more security from following seas a stern gate would offer a vessel of this type. Once loaded, the gate can be easily lowered with the ship underway. The gate would prevent following seas from boarding the stern of the boat. This feature would also confer more freedom of maneuver, with less pressure to keep the boat headed directly into a storm at all times.

Dwight Boyer reveals another serious problem with the *Marquette & Bessemer No. 2*. If his suspicions are correct, this, in combination with the open stern, would be disastrous in a major storm. "Study of the car-ferry's plans revealed that she had four hatches opening directly off the car deck. Two were for the coal bunkers and were always open and exposed. The other two led to the engine room and were protected only by a thin board covering." (Boyer)[xlvi] It takes no imagination at all to visualize a following sea swamping the car deck and flooding the engine room and coal bunkers. With her fires out and the ship dead in the water, she would be finished if the flooding didn't just outright sink her. If the ship were to begin to list, it is always possible that the load of rail cars may also have broken free, overwhelming the stern of the ship or causing her to roll. Interestingly, in addition to the ship never being found, reports of rail cars being found are

Museum Ship S.S. *City of Milwaukee.* **Author's Photo, 2015.**

limited. Most may still be lying on the cargo deck.

Museum ship *S.S City of Milwaukee*, **Manistee Michigan. Author's Photo, 2015.**
Note the stern gate.

One must appreciate that while a stern gate may be a vessel and
lifesaving piece of equipment, it would not make such a vessel impervious to
the weather. The *S.S. Milwaukee* was another car-ferry built by the American
Ship Building Company in Cleveland, Ohio in 1903. This vessel was
operated by the Grand Trunk Railroad and was lost in a savage storm on
Lake Michigan on Oct 22, 1929. There were no survivors and loss of life
estimates seem to range from 46 to 51 officers and crewman. This vessel was
equipped with a stern gate, and her car deck hatches were similar to manhole
covers dogged down with wedged locking devices. These were supposed to
be watertight. This ship was well-maintained ship and had been inspected
that year by both the Steamboat Inspection Service and the Grand Trunk
Railroad, receiving her certificate of seaworthiness. The *S.S. Milwaukee* was
drydocked in "June of 1926, May of 1927, and March of 1928. $33,332
($534,322 in today's dollars) was invested for repairs to the hull, rudders,
steering gear and propellers." (Boyer)[xlvii] Oddly, this vessel at this late date
was not equipped with wireless radio. She sailed into the unknown until the
wreck was discovered in 1972 in 120 feet of water about 3 miles off Fox Point
Wisconsin.

Five days after the sinking, the *S.S. Milwaukee*'s message case was found. The message, on Grand Trunk railway stationary in what was confirmed to be the Purser's handwriting reads as follows.

"S.S Milwaukee, October 22, '29 8:30 p.m. The ship is making water fast. We have turned around and headed for Milwaukee. Pumps are working, but sea gate is bent and can't keep the water out. Flicker is flooded. Seas are tremendous. Things look bad. Crew roll is about the same as on last pay day. (signed) A.R. Sadon, Purser."(Boyer)[xlviii]

The flicker is the crew compartment below the car deck and aft of the engine room. With the stern gate damaged, water was getting onto the car deck, but also the hatches were failing, or water was getting into the ship some other way. It is possible the hull was rocking and twisting so violently that the hatch covers were popped. More recent reports by divers also indicate that it is possible the proper hatch covers never existed in the first place, and there were indeed open hatchways to the lowest level of the ship. If so, the ship would have been much more easily flooded once the stern gate was damaged. Some of the rail cars on the wreck itself are also dislodged. In the end, while other ships stayed in port, the Milwaukee sailed into a brutal storm, succumbing to the violence of Lake Michigan. One wonders how the *Marquette & Bessemer No. 2*, trapped in a December storm without a stern gate or proper hatch covers, had any chance at all. It seems evident that neither the *Marquette & Bessemer No. 2* nor the S.S. Milwaukee should have been sailing on those days. In the case of the *Marquette & Bessemer No. 2*, sailing into a December blizzard was tempting fate.

The *S.S. Milwaukee* lost on Lake Michigan in 1929 seen here in happier days. Photo courtesy of the Father Edward J. Dowling, S.J. Marine Historical Collection of the University of Detroit Mercy Library.

Another danger which is a hazard to any railroad car ferry is the cargo itself. A load of upwards of 30 or more rail cars rests on the cargo deck on four lengths of railroad track. The cars may have different cargos with different weights and the boat must be loaded in such a way that the load is balanced. The strings of cars are held in place with jacks fastened to the rail, and sometimes chains and other restraints to keep the cars in place. In rough weather, these could fail, and the rail cars could break loose. This happened once on the No. 2, as recounted by the ship's former wheelsman, George Watts. Watts, who had sailed on the No. 2 for portions of 3 seasons, reported that once the jacks holding the rail cars in place did fail. "We were coming across with a load of cars, when the jacks holding two strings of cars gave way. They both started to rush out the end of the boat, but in some manner the two strings became wedged and held fast." (*The Evening Free Press*) [xlix] It was his belief that had the cars continued their trip toward the stern, the ship would have been doomed.

In the limited information available, it appears Captain Mcleod had other misgivings with the stability and seaworthiness of his ship. A Major Beattle was reached in Ottawa after the *Marquette & Bessemer No. 2* sank, and he recounted his trip as a passenger on the No. 2 the prior year. "It is nearly a year since I crossed the lake on the Bessemer. Hon. Mr. Hyman and a number of other gentlemen were with me. When we alighted on the dock here, I said: 'Well gentlemen, we have got back safely. But nothing under heaven could induce me to take that trip again.' When on the Bessemer, the major conversed with Capt. McLeod, who lost his life on the boat. Asked what would happen if the cars of coal were ever to shift, the captain said 'you will never hear of me again.' Major Beattle was convinced that this is exactly what happened." (Historical Collection of the Great Lakes-Bowling Green State University) [l] This was not the only report that Capt. McLeod had misgivings about the seaworthiness of his vessel.

"It is said that Capt. McLeod expected someday that the Bessemer would go down. It is said that she was top-heavy. She rolled terribly in an ordinary storm. One day last summer, she came into port with quite a sea on. The Bessemer was then rolling very badly. Capt. Walter Smith of London, who knew Capt. McLeod well, spoke of this to the commander and asked what caused it. 'The load is on the hurricane deck, not where it should be. That is what causes the rolling. If we were caught in a heavy storm and the cars shifted, a man would not have time to put on his hat until she was on the bottom.

She would go down like a shot.'" (*St Thomas Daily Times*)[liii]

Captain McLeod was not the only one to voice misgivings about the ship's stability in rough weather. Deckhand John Wirtz had mailed a letter to his family on the morning of December 7th, writing that the "vessel was a dangerous craft, unstable in rough weather, and that he had a constant fear for his life. This next trip will be my last." (Boyer)[liv] John Wirtz was lost with the rest of the officers and crew of the No. 2.

The hurricane deck is the cargo deck where the rail cars are loaded and stored. One can surmise that based on these passages, the cargo was stowed too high in the ship, making her top heavy and more prone to rolling and possibly capsizing. This deficit would be magnified in a fierce winter storm. Should ice accumulate on the superstructure and upper decks of the ship unevenly, that could also significantly enhance the prospects of the ship capsizing. We know that from the condition of the ships that survived this storm, icing was a huge problem, with some ships reporting they were so severely iced up that seeing out the pilothouse was severely impaired.

A much more blistering assessment was delivered in an editorial by P.C. Barkley, a former deep-water sailor. "That vessel could not be classed as seaworthy under any circumstances but was a ghastly man trap. That the boat had enormously high freeboard (distance from the water line to the upper deck) and no draft (distance between the water line and the keel). That a rush of water coming in through 'that great hole aft' must at once cause a list of a shift in the cargo. That a vessel of that design would roll over and founder if it fell into a trough of the waves, that the vessel was unable to ride her anchor in a gale and that she was doomed if her steering gear were disarranged." (Historical Collection of the Great Lakes)[lv] This statement supports commentary that I have read elsewhere that a ship of this construction with this much freeboard would have a very hard time successfully riding out a storm on her anchors, as the chains would likely snap under the strain, even when using the engines to take pressure off them. He further went on to say that the there is evidence the lifeboat was not equipped, and that "it should have reached shore in any gale with expert handling. That if the occupants of the lifeboat were sailors, they could have run the boat before the gale to safety." (Historical Collection of the Great Lakes)[lvi] We will discuss this more when we talk about the lifeboat itself.

The basic construction of the *Marquette & Bessemer No. 2* is similar to other carferries built by the American Shipbuilding Company. I have not, however, located any other information that implies the aforementioned issues were a problem specific to this design. I am not a marine engineer, nor do I claim to have any real knowledge in the area. I expect the height of the hurricane deck was dictated in part, by the rail docks the ship had to service. The draft of the vessel is similar to others built at the time, albeit probably shallow for a ship of that size. Perhaps other vessels were able to take on more ballast, allowing for a lower profile of the boat when underway. Perhaps the ship would have been heavier with a stern gate. That is merely speculation. As I have stated before, it is remarkable how some ships of this design went on to long, relatively trouble-free careers, while others met an untimely end. It should be noted, though, that both the *Marquette & Bessemer No. 2* and the S.S. *Milwaukee* were lost in terrible storms when they likely should have been in dock.

What is evident is that the only captain the ship ever had felt it was top-heavy, and that the ship was sufficiently prone to wild rolling that there were passengers who would not board the vessel again. One report made after the sinking indicates that Captain McLeod may have been contemplating a career change. A. E. Ponesford of St. Thomas was quoted as saying "Captain McLeod had expressed his interest in giving up command of the car ferry and embarking shortly on an enterprise of his own." (*St. Thomas Daily Times*)[lvii] Whether this statement related to the lack of a stern gate or other deficiencies of the ship, a man seeking new opportunities, or merely a change of lifestyle, we will never know. If we couple this with the Achilles heel of the ship not being fitted with a stern gate plus Boyer's theory that the car deck hatches had little to no protection from boarding seas, one could conclude that the vessel had no chance of survival on the night of that savage storm on December 7.th The weather that night went from bad to worse, with winds reaching 70 miles an hour, inches of snow, terrible visibility and crushing waves. It is evident that despite their reputation for sturdiness and power, a ship that was used basically as an all-weather ship that was even a good ice breaker, the early car ferries did have some design weaknesses.

Note that not all agreed the rail cars breaking loose may have contributed to the loss. "Fireman Nicholson, who was with Captain McLeod (John?) on the *Shenango* reported 'I do not believe that the boat was lost through one of the strings of cars giving way and causing the boat to list. While there was always a danger of such a thing happening, they were always prepared with extra wedges, and when the cars showed any signs of giving way, each car was jacked up securely. If anything did happen, one of the two middle strings would have to go first as the two on the outside ran off switches from the centre and any break away would merely result in a pile up in the stern.' Nicholson further went on to say that it would be next to impossible to ship enough water through the open stern to sink her as it would splash in and run through the drains built for that purpose." (St. Thomas Daily Times)[lviii] After the flooding episode in the month before the ship's sinking, I am not certain Captain McLeod would have agreed with him.

As mentioned, previously, the cars apparently did have the capability to break free. George Watts, a wheelsman on the car ferry for parts of three seasons recounts such a terrifying event. "One time, we were coming across the lake with a load of cars when the jacks holding two strings of cars gave way. They both started to rush out the end of the boat, but in some manner, the two strings became wedged and held fast. Only for that it would have been all up for us." (The Evening Free Press)[lix]

I feel this information is relevant to our story. First, it gives us a very reasonable cause for the loss of the Marquette & Bessemer No. 2. I am prepared to speculate that we can make two other conclusions from this information. Given some of the ship's failings and the horrific weather of December 7th, it seems reasonable to speculate that the ship probably sank early in the storm despite the eyewitness reports to the contrary. This was my initial impression. I believe it is only the skill and experience of the ship's crew and officers that may have kept the ship afloat later into the storm. This is relevant when we get to the many different sightings and reports of the vessel later in the story. Some reports of the ship's whistle were as late as Thursday morning. I believe the No. 2 was on the bottom of the lake by then, but we will never know the exact timing of the sinking for certain.

This information may help us narrow down its location and what she was attempting to do. The next bit of speculation is that when the ship did founder, it sank very quickly. This idea is supported by other information we will discuss when we get to the physical evidence of the loss, particularly that we can confirm only one lifeboat was successfully launched from the ship. Its occupants did not have proper clothing or other gear for the weather and it appears the lifeboat was launched under great duress.

The No. 2 underway outside Conneaut Harbor. Photo courtesy of the Richard Wright Collection, Great Lakes Marine Collection. Historical Collection of the Great Lakes, Bowling Green State University

Chapter Three: The Crew

**Photo courtesy of the Historical Collections of the Great Lakes,
Bowling Green State University.**

Above is a rare, to my knowledge, never published photo of some of
the crew of the *Marquette & Bessemer No. 2*. It is undated and appears to be
taken at the same time as some of the others when the ship was being freed
from pack ice. None of the sailors in this photo are identified; however, it is
likely that some of them were onboard the No. 2 when she sank.

The crew of the No. 2 was a fairly diverse cross-section of society in
terms of economic class. One major draw to serving on the No. 2 was the
quick turnaround that allowed officers and crewman to establish a home
and the ability to actually spend time there. Most who worked Great Lakes
ships would depart in the spring and rarely see home again until the shipping
season ended. The No. 2 had the advantage of being back in its home port
most nights. The crew list indicates that many of the crew called Conneaut,
Ohio home. Many others were from Ontario. The storm of December
1909 was an especially painful event for Conneaut because so many of the
crew made their homes there. Crew lists were always a little fluid in 1909.
Some crew members might miss a sailing, or a new person might be added.
This fluctuation was likely especially true for the more demanding or less
attractive jobs on the ship. Still the core of the No. 2's crew roster appeared
to be stable with limited fluctuations.

The Crew of the Marquette & Bessemer No. 7

Officers	R.R. McLeod, Captain, Conneaut, Ohio J.C. McLeod, First mate, Courtright, Ontario Frank Stone, Second mate, Conneaut Ohio R. C. Smith, Purser, Conneaut, Ohio G.R. Smith, Steward, Conneaut, Ohio Eugene Wood, Chief engineer, Conneaut, Ohio E. Buckler, First assistant, Conneaut, Ohio T. Kennedy, Second engineer, Conneaut, Ohio
Firemen	F. Steele, Conneaut, Ohio J. F. Shank, Conneaut, Ohio W. Wigglesworth, Conneaut, Ohio
Wheelsmen	W. Wilson, Conneaut, Ohio Fred Walker, unknown
Watchmen	F. Annis, Conneaut, Ohio J. Clancy, Cleveland, Ohio
Cooks	H. Thomas, second cook, Port Stanley, Ontario J. W. (Manny) Sauers, waiter, Conneaut, Ohio G. Lawrence, porter, Port Stanley, Ontario
Coal Passers	R. Hines, Canada (also appears spelled as Hinds) Charles Allen, Renovo, Pennsylvania P. Keith, Conneaut, Ohio J. King, Port Stanley, Ontario Wm. Ray, Conneaut, Ohio J. O'Hagan, London, Ontario J. Bailey, Canada
Seamen	F. Barrett, Wisconsin E. Harvey, unknown P. Hughes, Conneaut, Ohio D. Ball, unknown Charles Crutts, unknown
Oilers	J. Wirtz, Detroit, Michigan J. Hart, Conneaut, Ohio

Above is the crew roster as listed in the *Conneaut New-Herald* after the ship's loss and is probably as accurate a list as is available. (*Conneaut News-Herald*)[lx]
D. Ball is listed here as unknown, but he was a resident of Simcoe or St. Thomas, Ontario. Note that some of the lists reported do not exactly match,

and there may have been crew members added at the last minute.

A crew list published in the London, Ontario newspaper lists a couple names not included above. These are M. Sharp, J. Olsen, R Reid, and J. Schwartz, all listed as address unknown. (*The Evening Free Press*) Were all or some of these men late additions to the *Bessemer* crew, perhaps joining the boat in Port Stanley? We may never know for sure. It is a topic that merits further research but falls outside the scope of my book. The uncertainty of crew lists reflects what life was like on the ships in 1909.

This list accounts for 32 crew and officers, including oiler John Wirtz, who planned to leave the boat after this trip. Not included in this list is Mr. Albert Weiss of the Keystone Fish company. You may recall Mr. Weiss as the unlucky soul who just barely made the boat as it was leaving harbor. In the accounts of the loss of the ship, the number of lives lost has varied a bit between 32 and 36. It seems likely that there was a bit of short-term turnover in some positions on this ship. This was likely commonplace with ships all over the lake as some of the jobs were probably casual, with people coming and going on ships throughout the season. The impact of the strike, plus late season operations, may have contributed to crew scarcity at many ports on the Great Lakes. The core of the crew, however, was stable. Much of the crew and all of the officers appear to have been in their respective positions for some time. A small portion of the crew had much less experience. It is striking that in this listing, the home towns of some of the crew members were reported to be unknown. Some of the crew came from other walks of life, and some were life-long sailors. Anecdotes and brief stories about the crew and their personalities are recounted better in Boyer's book than I could ever hope to do here. Regardless, it would be remiss to ignore some information that is available regarding the officers and crew of the ship who helped shape the story.

As we move into this section of the book, recall Captain Driscoll's account of the recovery of the No. 4 lifeboat that opened the book. . Although the ship was lost with all hands, bodies were recovered and some of the internment information is listed in this section as well as in Chapter 6. The recovery of lifeboat No. 4 is covered in much greater detail in Chapter 5.

Following are the obituaries of some of crew of the No. 2 that appeared in the *Erie Times-News* shortly after the ship's loss. (*Erie Times-News*)[lxii] These obituaries give us at least an overview of who these men were. Information about some of the other crew members was a bit scattered and more difficult to find, and not all the crewman were listed in the *Erie-Times News*. This is especially true of some Canadian members of the crew, whose obituaries may have appeared in their local papers. I have reproduced the *Erie-Times* obits here, replete with all their original errors in some cases.

R.R. McLeod

"Robert R. McLeod, captain, was born October 3, 1862, at Kincardine, Ontario (another article lists his date of birth as October 2nd). He went on the lakes at the age of 12 years old and for 35 years, had never missed a season. After serving in various minor capacities and through all the grades of seamanship, he became captain of the steamer Osceola, then of the Colorado and later of the Ann Arbor No.1. He was married on the 22nd of December 1886 at Duluth, Minnesota, to Miss Murdine Martin, who survives. Three daughters also survive, Miss Belle, Lulu, and Roberta. He removed to Conneaut in 1895 and had since continuously sailed of this port. He was captain for a time of the Shenango No.1, then of the Grand Haven, sailed the Collier No.1 (Marquette & Bessemer No.1) on her first trip out of this port and then took over the No. 2, taking her out on her first trip in 1903 (*error, ship built in 1905*) and remaining with her throughout the six (*error, 4 years*) years she sailed Lake Erie. He was a member of the Masonic fraternity of the Maccabees and of the Woodmen of the World leaving life insurance in the latter two. He leaves five living brothers, all sailors, and an aged mother and two sisters." (*Erie-Times News*)[lxiii]

Captain McLeod was widely regarded as an excellent captain with a long history of impeccable service on the Great Lakes. No one had a bad word to say about him, and to include all the people who had glowing praise for the man would make this chapter much larger than I intended. Below are some of the reports supporting this thesis.

"I served as a pilot with Captain McLeod on Lake Michigan," said Captain Stephens. "He was in command of the car ferry Grand Haven, which carried cars across the lake from Milwaukee to Grand Haven. He is one of the best navigators on the lakes and has a good reputation everywhere. I've seen him in some tight pinches and he always came out alright." (*The Evening Free Press*)[lxiv]

Fireman Nicholson said that he served with Captain McLeod on some of the fiercest gales on Lake Erie (He reports serving with Captain McLeod on the *Shenango* for ten months) and that he was one of the best mariners on the lakes. (*The Evening Free Press*)[lxv]

Another former crewman has praised the captain. George Watts was a wheelsman for parts of three seasons with Captain McLeod. "We were out in much heavy weather and we had a good many close calls. Working as a wheelsman close to McLeod, I came to know him very well, and I want to say that he was one of the very best, both as a seaman and a man." (*The Evening Free Press*)[lxvi] Captain Robert Rowan McLeod is buried at the City Cemetery in Conneaut, Ohio. There is a grave marker. (*Historical Collection of the Great Lakes*)[lxvii]

Captain Robert McLeod inset. Post Card Courtesy of the Richard J. Wright Great Lakes Marine Collection. Historical Collection of the Great Lakes, Bowling Green State University.

John McLeod

First mate, was born about the year 1868 (*This reported date of birth is an obvious error as John was purported to be 60 years old at the time of the sinking and was the oldest of the McLeod brothers. In Donna McLeod Rodebaugh's unpublished family history and elsewhere, John is reported to have been born in February of 1853 in Kincardine, Ontario*). He went on the Great Lakes in 1864 and had seen continuous service for the forty-five years intervening. His present home was at Courtright, Ontario, he having removed there some years ago, after having been a resident of Conneaut for a couple of years. He was twice married, his last wife being Miss Mary Scanion of Sarnia, Canada, to whom he was married in 1887. She survives him with eight children, two by the former marriage, his mother, five brothers and two sisters. He was a member of the Knights of Columbus and of the C.M.B.A (Catholic Mutual Benefits Association?), with whom he had life insurance. During his nearly half century on the Lakes he had served on a large number of boats. Since Conneaut knowledge of him, he had been captain of the old *Shenango No. 1* and was at the time of the latter burning in the local harbor seven years ago. He then went as captain of the New York.

When his brother, Capt. Robert McLeod took over the car ferry, he returned as first mate and had been continuously with her until she went down. (*Erie-Times News*)[lxviii]

"John McLeod had recently acquired some farmland in Courtright Ontario (moving?) from Conneaut Ohio after marrying a girl from Sarnia Ontario. He was hopeful his brother Hugh, who was captain of a laid-up Pittsburgh Steamship Company steamer, would be able to relieve him for a few trips so he could attend to details, chores and taxes. Hugh McLeod's employer would not release him, however." (Boyer)[lxix] John McLeod is buried at the Our Lady of Mercy Cemetery in Sarnia, Ontario. There is a headstone." (Historical Collection of the Great Lakes)[lxx]

Eugene Wood

Chief Engineer, aged 40 years, came to this city 12 years ago from Port Duluth, Ontario, where he was born and raised. He accepted a position as assistant engineer under George Coillinge of this city and two years later, when Mr. Coillinge resigned his position as chief engineer on one of the ferry boats, Mr. Wood was advanced to fill the vacancy. Practically the entire ten years that he has served he has been with Captain McLeod. Lake men say that there was no better engineer on the lakes than was he. About nine years ago he was married to Miss Gertrude Rensal of Ashtabula. The wife and two children, Mildred aged seven and George, aged five, survive. He has a sister and a brother living. (*Erie-Times News*)[lxxi] Wood's brother was master of the steamer *Bannockburn*, lost with all hands-on Lake Superior in 1902. (Boyer)[lxxii] The *Bannockburn* has never been found, and it has been it has been reportedly seen on the water since its disappearance. Eugene Wood is buried in St. John's Cemetery in St. Catherine's, Ontario. The grave is marked. (Historical Collection of the Great Lakes)[lxxiii]

Frank E. Stone

Second Mate, was born in Vermillion, Ohio, July 11th, 1884, and removed with his parents Mr. and Mrs. L.V. Stone to Conneaut about a year later. He had resided here continuously since that time. He went through the primary and grammar grades of the local schools and through the first two years of high school. He then went into his father's jewelry store where he spent five years learning the business and became a master jeweler. Three years ago, he was made purser of the car ferry and continued in that office for two years and a half. During that period, he accomplished a remarkable feat of having never missed a trip. Last winter he took the mate and pilot examination and, on being successful, was this summer promoted to second mate of the ferry. He was the youngest man on the lakes, holding a full commission as pilot. He was for a time an officer of the Hook & Ladder Fire company of this city and joined Company L of the Ohio National Guard, when it was organized, rising the rank of second lieutenant. He was a member of the Masonic fraternity and of the Methodist Church (*Erie-Times News*).[lxxiv] "Stone had been on the job a little over three months, succeeding Charles Myers who had left for a similar job on the *Ashtabula*." (Boyer)[lxxv] Frank Stone was never married, and his body is not thought be among the 14 that were recovered.

R.C. Smith

Purser, was born in about the year 1882. He came to Conneaut in September to accept the position held at the time of his death. He followed the lakes for a number of years, giving up his position on the Ashtabula car ferry when he accepted the one here. He was married to Ida Wheeler of Stratford Ont., five years ago, one child, however, aged 2 years resulting from the union. The family moved here from Ashtabula the middle of September, making their home at 454 Washington street extension. (*Erie-Times News*)[lxxvi] Purser Smith was not thought to be among the 14 confirmed bodies that have been recovered from the *Marquette & Bessemer No. 2*.

Edward Buckler

First Assistant Chief, was 33 years of age. He was on the ferry No. 1 (probably the collier, but could be referring to the *Shenango*) when that boat was brought out and brought out the ferry on which he sailed to his death (Buckler was with both boats on their maiden voyage). He worked with Eugene Wood for the last eight years. Mr. Buckler was formerly from Marine City, as is his wife, who resides at 542 Harbor Street. There are four little children, Beatrice, aged ten, Avery, aged 8, George, aged 3, and a babe three months old. He also leaves four brothers and two sisters. (*Erie-Times News*) [lxxvii] Buckler's body is not thought to be one of those recovered. He was likely serving in the engine room at the time of the ship's sinking.

Thomas Kennedy

Second Engineer born in the year 1878, came to Conneaut 11 years ago from a little Michigan town. He at once took a position on the lakes, working under the direction of Eugene Wood as chief engineer. He was a member of the car ferry crew when it was brought out four years ago. Five years ago, last May he was wedded to Miss Minnie Lehman of Rosebush, Mich. There are no children. (*Erie-Times News*)[lxxviii] There is a grave marker for Thomas Kennedy in the Riverside Cemetery in Mount Pleasant, Michigan, but I do not believe his body was ever recovered. (Historical Collection of the Great Lakes)[lxxix]

Note here that in all the accounts I have read regarding this loss, Captain McLeod is always praised and was regarded as both a very competent captain and an individual of very high character. Captain McLeod was well-regarded on both sides of the lake and had many friends in Conneaut, Port Stanley and St. Thomas. The same is said of his very experienced group of officers. John McLeod was serving as first mate of the vessel, but also held his captain's license and had served on other boats and Eugene Wood was always described as a very capable engineer who was regarded as good as any serving on the lakes. Frank Stone was a man of obvious and diverse talents who apparently was something of a prodigy. *The Marquette & Bessemer No. 2* had experienced, qualified officers.

John Hart*

Oiler, known by everyone by the nickname of "Paddy," was a typical follower of the sea. His home was anyplace his boat happened to be. During the past six years, he has been on the car ferry and has made his home here the greater part of the time. "Paddy" came from Ireland when he was a boy. He was reported to be a member of the Col. Lynch brigade that left

Chicago at the time of the South African war to help the Boars and he delighted in telling his fellow sailors of the experiences he had while fighting under Col. Lynch. He was about 38 years of age. (Erie-Times News) [lxxx] Hart was one of the more experienced crewmen on the ship. John Hart is buried in the Trinity Cemetery in Erie, Pennsylvania. There is no marker. (Historical Collection of the Great Lakes)[lxxxi]

Patrick Keith

Coal passer, aged about 35 years was another typical sailor. He was known to quite an extent by harbor businessmen, making Conneaut his staying place during the greater part of last year. For nearly six months, Keith tried to secure a position on the car ferry and was only successful about a month ago. It is not believed that he has any relatives living. (Erie-Times News) [lxxii] Keith appears to have had limited experience as a sailor, but it is not completely clear. Apparently, he had been with the boat for only about a month. Patrick Keith's body was recovered, floating about 3 miles off Port Colborne, Ontario in late April of 1910. His body was identified by a distinctive scar over his eye. It is unclear where he is buried.

P. Hughes

Seaman, aged about 45 years, has been with the car ferry since the boat first came out. His home is in Michigan and all of his relatives reside there. For the four years that he has been employed there, he has made Conneaut his home. He had been with the car ferry since her launch in 1905. (Erie Times-News)[lxxxiii] Hughes is another of the seamen who have a great deal of experience. It is not believed his body was among those recovered.

Charles Croutts

Seaman, aged 25 years, came here three years ago from Aberdeen, Scotland, where he was born and raised. He had been working on the ferry No. 2 for about three months. All of his relatives reside in the old country, except one brother, who is thought to be in St. Louis. (Erie-Times News) [lxxiv] It was subsequently revealed in a letter that arrived in Conneaut that Charles was the sole support of his invalid father, mother and sister back in Aberdeen, Scotland. The family was in destitute circumstances, spending their last five dollars on coal and facing eviction. This was brought to the attention of the Elks and a money order for $35.00 was raised to help his family. (Conneaut News-Herald)[lxxxv]

It is not believed his body was among those recovered.

Charles Allen*

Coal passer aged about 18 years, was born and raised in Renovo, PA. He came to Conneaut a year ago, accepting a position with the Conneaut Company. He was an expert barber and for a time conducted a shop at the harbor. Indoor work, however, was very injurious to his health and for this reason about a month ago, he went to work on the car ferry boat. He leaves a mother, two sisters and two brothers. (*Erie-Times News*) Allen appears to have been another of the more inexperienced hands on the crew, with only a limited amount of time on the ship. He was one of the youngest members of the crew. An experienced barber would be a welcome addition amongst any ship's crew. (Boyer). Charles Allen is buried in the North Bend Cemetery in North Bend, Pennsylvania. (Historical Collection of the Great Lakes)[lxxv]

Tom Steele*

Fireman, aged 24 years, was born and raised in Edinburgh, Scotland, and came to this country three years ago, making Conneaut his home. He sailed for about two seasons on the car ferry No. 2 and his friends believe, from things that he said, that the trip on which he met his death was to have been his last one on the boat. He leaves a father and mother, Mr. and Mrs. John Steele, Carnegie Street, and a brother and sister. His body was among those found in the yawl boat. (*Erie Times-News*) Thomas Steele is buried in St. Joseph's cemetery in Conneaut, Ohio and he has a headstone. (Historical Collection of the Great Lakes)

Joe Schenk*

Fireman, aged about 25 years, has made Conneaut his home for the last three years. Switzerland is his native country, and he came to America only a few years ago. After serving a season as a member of a cable gang at the harbor, he accepted a position on the ferry and has been employed on that boat for two seasons. He recently took a vacation trip, returning to his old position on the boat just 15 days before the fatal trip. Joe Schenk (often appears in articles as Shank) is buried near Paddy Hart in an unmarked grave at Trinity Cemetery in Erie, Pennsylvania. (Historical Collection of the Great Lakes)

George Smith *

Steward, was born in the year 1876. His early home was at Ladner, B.C., and when but a lad of about 13 years, he took to the lakes and made his livelihood up until the time of his death by following the water. About ten years ago he was united in marriage to Anna Narconne, of Detroit, who still survives. He also leaves two children, George, aged 7, and James, aged 5, a father and mother and three brothers. (*Erie Times-News*)[xcii] George Smith is buried in City Cemetery in Conneaut, Ohio. There is a headstone. (Historical Collection of the Great Lakes)[xciii]

Frank Annis

Watchman, aged 48 years, had been a member of the crew of the car ferry for two seasons. He was born in Pomfret township, New York state, and resided in the vicinity of Conneaut during the past ten years. One daughter, Laura Annis, aged 22, resides in Cleveland. Also leaves a brother and a sister. Mr. Annis was employed by the Bessemer for a time and while in the employ of that company, invented a rail chair, a device designed to replace fish plates. (*Conneaut News-Herald*)[xciv] There is a grave marker for Frank Annis in Oak Hill Cemetery in Pontiac, Michigan, however his body is not thought to be among those recovered. (Historical Collection of the Great Lakes)[xcv]

J.W. Souars*

Waiter, aged 20 years, was born in Portugal and at the age of 6 years moved with his family to this country. For 12 years he has resided in Conneaut and has many friends at the harbor among the young people. Since he was 16 years of age he has been sailing on the lakes, this being his second season on the ferry. He has a father and mother, Mr. and Mrs. Joe Souars, Lake Road, and four brothers. Apparently Souars is an incorrect spelling, and the correct spelling of the last name appears to be Soares. While he is reported to be born in Portugal, his death certificate lists his birthplace as Italy. He was reported by Boyer to be one of the most popular men in the crew. He is buried at the St. Joseph Cemetery in Conneaut, Ohio. (Historical Collection of the Great Lakes)[xcvi]

Joseph O'Hagen

I am not completely clear on O'Hagen or as it often appears, O' Hagan. He is a bit of a mystery man. He is on some lists of crews as a coal passer that was on the ferry when she left Tuesday morning. There are several variations of the spelling of his name. At one point, he was mistaken to be one of the men on lifeboat No. 4. (*Cleveland Plain Dealer*)[xcvii] He was also reported as not on the ferry. "By telegram received in Conneaut yesterday from W.H. Jenkins, local agent for the Seaman's Union, who was in Cleveland yesterday trying to locate relatives of William Wilson, discovered that Joseph O'Hagan, reported as among the coal passers on the car ferry when she left Tuesday morning, was not on the ferry when she left Tuesday." (*Erie Times-News*)[xcviii] I do not think we will ever know for sure if O'Hagen was on the boat. I have not been able to find out much more about this mysterious individual.

John King

Coal Passer, appears to have been born about 1884 which would have made him 23 when he was serving aboard the No. 2. He was Born in Liverpool, England and arrived in Canada in 1907. "He comes of a seafaring family, and has had several relatives lost at sea. Had a premonition of possible disaster. Filled with a premonition that the ship would be lost, and realizing that from his great-grandfather on down his race had paid tribute to the mighty deep, he returned to London two weeks ago, and although warned by a family member and friends not to go back, he returned to Port Stanley and shipped out again." (Historical Collection of the Great Lakes)[xcix] He was the only known crewmember from London, Ontario and had worked as a laborer and sailor. He had only been with the Bessemer about 6 weeks. He joins several others in the crew who were relative new additions and who also appear to have had a sense of foreboding regarding the ship.

William "Ed" Harvey

Seaman, was only 19 years old at the time of the No. 2 sinking. I have not been able to determine his hometown, although he may have been from Port Stanley, Ontario.

With a couple limited exceptions, I have reproduced these obituaries as they appeared in the *Erie-Times*. A couple things stand out. There is a propensity of the copywriter to write in run on sentences. There were a few other typographical errors, but I have attempted to reproduce them as they originally appeared. Other things that stood out were how little information was available about some crew members. In some cases, only approximate ages were known. This was especially true of the ordinary crewman, some of which had not been with the ship for more than a season, or in some cases, a matter of weeks. Some were relatively new immigrants to the United States. Many of the officers and crew had connections to both the USA and Canada. The nature of the ship's regular trip between Ohio and Ontario would have been attractive to men with roots in both countries. Many had worked the lakes for decades, and it is striking that several began their careers working on the lakes as children by today's standards.

As I stated earlier, some of the information about the other crew members was more difficult to come by and was sometimes contradictory. In other situations, obituaries were listed in the crewman's hometown, when known. Crew members also hailed from Canada, Michigan, Pennsylvania, New York, and other parts of Ohio. Some of these are listed as follows.

W. Wrigglesworth

Appears to be Rene Wrigglesworth. As reported in the St. Thomas Daily Times on Dec 13, 1909, Rene lived in New Sarum, Ontario with a brother-in-law, James Gillard. He expressed great reluctance at having to go back to the boat. He had been a fireman on the boat for four years, was about 22 years old and was originally born in Norwich (England?). It was said he was well liked by all who knew him. (St Thomas Daily Times)[c] With four years on the job, Rene was one of the more experienced amongst the regular crew. He too, like several of his peers, expressed some apprehension returning to the boat.

D. Ball

Appears to be Earl Ball and had just turned 19 right before the No. 2 sank. It appears he had only been with the boat three weeks. He had five brothers and two sisters. Reports are he had a brother who had just been hospitalized for seven weeks with typhoid fever about the time of the sinking and that 4 family members had met violent ends in the last 20 years. It can be inferred that he was a resident of St. Thomas, but this is unclear. (Simcoe Reformer)[ci]

D. Ball's mother wrote a heartfelt letter after the sinking that was printed in the Conneaut News-Herald. I reproduce in its entirety here.

"Simcoe, Ontario, December 14, 1909, Postmaster, Conneaut, Ohio

Dear Sir, I am writing a few lines of sympathy with the mothers who have lost sons and wives who have lost husbands in the sinking of the boat Bessemer No. 2, as my son was one of the crew who went down with it. This was his first year on the lake. He was only 19 years of age. His brothers John and Thomas both sailed on the boat last year.

This makes four out of the Ball family that have met sudden deaths. This young man's father was killed eight years ago while engaged in harbor improvement work at Port Burwell. If the body of my boy is recovered, please notify me at once. I hope they will find all of the poor fellows who gave up their lives in this disaster. What suffering they must have endured.

Yours truly, Mrs. John Garland"

(Conneaut News-Herald)[cii]

This letter reflects a family that has endured great loss. Work was dangerous and could be brutal in 1909.

Harry Thomas*

"Second Cook, was from Port Stanley, Ontario and was 22 years of age and had lived here all his life. There is at home besides his parents, two brothers, Ernest and Nell, the latter being a teacher at the Balaclava Steet School. Harry was a member of the Methodist Church and the I.O.O.F. He was home last Monday, the last time the boat was in. He was intending to leave the boat at Christmas and had his plans laid out for the future." (St. Thomas Daily Times)[ciii] Harry Thomas is buried at the United Union Church Cemetery. He has a headstone. (Historical Collection of the Great Lakes)[civ]

William H. Ray*

Oiler, appears to have been born February 21st, 1884, in Butler, PA. A photograph of him appears in the *Butler Times* on December 15th, 1909. William was the son of a former police chief. He felt unsafe and did not like the lake business, telling his father he would seek work on land. Unfortunately, he never got that opportunity. It was reported that this was his first trip on the car-ferry. (*The Evening Free Press*)[cv] "It was his first trip on the boat, and he was nervous. He had been employed on one of the dock's ore unloaders during the summer, but the season was ending, and the opening on the car ferry black gang roster was his for the asking." (Boyer)[cvi]

It is believed William Ray is buried in Butler, Pennsylvania, but this detail is not completely clear.

46

F. Barret

Seaman, appears on the crew list as from Wisconsin. He may have been born in Ireland in 1875, making him 34 years old or so at the time of the No. 2's sinking. I have not been able to find out a great deal more about this gentleman. He is not confirmed to be among the bodies recovered from the car ferry.

J. Bailey

Coal passer, appears to have been born in Canada and was about 26 to 27 years old. Little more is known, and it appears his body was not among those recovered.

John Clancy

Watchman, appears to have been born about 1868, possibly in Michigan. He was listed in living in Cleveland, Ohio in 1908 and was unmarried. He would have been about 40 or 41 years old at the time of the No. 2's loss and had a brother named Daniel and a sister Sarah, who reported she saw the boat go down in a dream. (*Flint Journal*)[cvii] "Two Cleveland men, M. Clancy and B. Thompson, searched Long Point looking for survivors, trekking 30 miles along the beach, finding only a portion of a lifeboat and other wreckage, but no survivors or bodies." (Historical Collection of the Great Lakes)[cviii] It does not appear that his body was recovered.

John Wirtz

Oiler, born December 10, 1869, in Saginaw, Michigan. "Wirtz was the son of the late George Wirtz, one of Saginaw's most prominent citizens. He was a machinist on the *Marquette & Bessemer* and was a resident of Saginaw nearly all his life. Wirtz was 38 and was a widower, with a daughter Edna living in Detroit. He has a sister, Mrs. Geo W. Stewart, wife of Saginaw's mayor." (*The Flint Journal*)[cix]

John Wirtz also had misgivings about the car ferry. Wirtz wrote his family about a week before the ship's last trip that "the ferry was a dangerous craft, unstable in rough weather, and that he had constant fear for his life. The next trip will be my last. I am going to leave the ferry boat then and seek other employment. Wirtz told of an accident to the *Marquette & Bessemer* only a short time ago, in which the boat rocked badly in a storm, nearly turned turtle. The boat shifted its load of cars and nearly capsized before they could be back into place. (Historical Collection of the Great Lakes)[cx]

John Wirtz does not appear to be among those recovered from the wreck.

Roy Hines*

Coal Passer, St. Thomas, Ontario. Roy Hines funeral service was performed in conjunction with that of Harry Thomas by Reverend E.G. Powell. His body, recovered in lifeboat No. 4, was originally identified as O'Hagan. Roy Hines is buried in the Union United Church Cemetery in Union, Ontario. There is no headstone. (Historical Collection of the Great Lakes)[cxi]

Indicates this was one of the crew members recovered in lifeboat No.4

In addition to the crew, we must account for the late arriving passenger, Mr. Albert J. Weis. Mr. Weis was the treasurer of the Bay State Iron Works and the Keystone Fish Company. He was a well-known local businessman in Erie, Pa who is survived by his wife and two sons. (Erie Times-News)[cxii]

Not mentioned in many of the lists of the lost is the possibility of a second passenger. I have not seen it written anywhere that he was confirmed to be on the ship, however, in the Monday, Dec 13th, 1909 edition of the Erie Times-News, his name appears.

"It is also feared that Crist Johnson, 321 West Fourth street, was on the ill-fated boat. He was supposed to make the trip from Conneaut to Port Stanley on Tuesday and his friends have not heard from him since that time." (Erie Times News)[cxiii] It appears the man simply vanished. He was likely on the car ferry when she went down. Little of him is written, however.

Another man that was not on the above crew list, but who may very well have been on the boat was a man named O.T.W. Lander. Lander has appeared on some other crew lists. When the Marquette & Bessemer's No. 4 lifeboat was recovered, clothing frozen to the bottom of the boat along with a $5.00 dollar bill was recovered. There was "a note for $10.00 payable to Harry Schmidt, Conneaut and signed by O.T.W. Lander near the $5.00 dollar bill." (Cleveland Plain Dealer)[cxiv] It has been speculated that the extra set of clothing found in the bottom of the boat belonged to a tenth crewman who jumped from the boat and that that man may have been O.T.W. Lander. Little is reported about this individual, but he may have been one of the crewmen on the No. 2 on its final trip.

Three men who missed the boat and were not on it that horrific trip include Michael Haruch (I have also seen it spelled Staruck), George Lawrence, and Tom Cleaver. Michael Haruch had been hospitalized as a result of injuries he had suffered while working on the boat two weeks earlier. "Michael, who is a native of Poland, and speaks very little English, was employed as a fireman on the car ferry. On Monday, he fell down an open hatchway and fractured his skull. Capt. McLeod, skipper of the boat, who is a friend of Dr. Guest of this city communicated with the latter and arranged to have the man sent to St. Thomas to the Aman Wood hospital in a special coach attached to a Pere Marquette train." (*St. Thomas Daily Times*)[cxv] Michael must have made out okay and recovered sufficiently to return to duty. In a subsequent article, "He will be sailing on the Per Marquette No. 19 that is to take the place of the lost steamer." In this article, he is listed as one of the No. 2's officers. (*Erie Times-News*)[cxvi] He did not appear on the crew list at the time of the loss, which makes sense as he was injured and probably not on the payroll list. I suspect the *Erie Times-News* listing of the man as an officer is probably incorrect if he spoke little English, and that his true position on the boat was fireman.

George Lawrence is on the list of the No. 2's crew who missed the trip. Apparently, the ship was short crewmen, including a fireman and a coal passer and George Lawrence was sent to recruit a couple of men. Fortunately for him, he was not able to locate anyone on the streets of Port Stanley. Not only did not get any crewman, but he missed the boat's departure from Port Stanley, Ontario on December 6th, thus, sparing his life. George Lawrence was listed as a porter on the No. 2. (Historical Collection of the Great Lakes) [cxvii]

Tom Cleaver was an oiler with the boat, who suddenly decided to forsake a sailor's life and went to work as a porter in a hotel. (*The Evening Free Press*)[cxviii] Another with impeccable timing was William Tyler, who left the boat 2 trips before its sinking and reported to his brother that he was actually in Cleveland and not on the Bessemer at the time of its sinking. (*St. Thomas Journal*)[cxix]

Good fortune smiled on these individuals and shows how little things can have an outsized impact on one's life. Granted, a fractured skull is no small affair, but it turned out to be fortuitous for Michael Haruch. Just as these men were fortunate, Mr. Albert Weis was unfortunate in making the dock at the last minute. It is clear many of the men had misgivings about making this trip, including probably Captain McLeod. It is also clear that

Captain McLeod's biggest error in judgement was ultimately sailing in the first place, although he could not have foreseen the incredible deterioration in weather conditions. Many other captains had to make the same choice and some paid dearly. Such was the pressure to sail and deliver cargo in 1909.

Many of those who did survive this storm had experiences that could generously be described as harrowing. It took nerve to sail in December. In the end, we will probably never know fully the accurate crew list at the time of the sinking.

Above is the iconic picture of the *Marquette & Besemer No. 2* using dynamite to clear the ship from the ice. This photo was made into a post card and was taken in Conneaut, Ohio, but the date is unclear. Post Card courtesy of the Ivan Brookes Collection. Historical Collection of the Great Lakes, Bowling Green State University.

Chapter Four: Sailing Into a Frozen Hell

Weather was already ominous as the *Marquette & Bessemer No. 2* left Conneaut harbor two hours behind schedule. Captain McLeod and the crew were already coming off one of the most harrowing crossings they had ever experienced. As previously written, the ship's departure was already delayed 2 hours by winds so severe that it broke a freighter free from its winter moorings. Several vessels working on the harbor fog signal were being kicked about by strong wind gusts and storm signals were up as the No. 2 was seen leaving the harbor at 10:43 AM. "As the car ferry, making steam and passing by the site and began making seas, Captain McLeod, standing on the flying-bridge wing, his oilskins and sou'wester flapping in the wind, yelled over to the crew working on the new fog signal. 'Get that thing fixed,' he shouted. 'I may need it on my way back.' " (Boyer)[cxx]

A few miles from the harbor, an inbound fishing tug, the *Alberta T*, reported seeing the car ferry as well. By then the winds were already climbing and the temperature was dropping. A severe southwest gale with winds up to 70 miles an hour was about to reign chaos on both land and lake, knocking down wires and plastering the area in snow. One of the worst storms in years was about to strike the lake, taking a brutal toll. "The steamer *Clarion* ran aground and caught fire. 15 lives were lost and six were saved. The *W.C. Richardson* ran aground on Waverly Shoal outside Buffalo with a loss of five (eight in later reports) lives. The *Josiah G. Munro* ran aground attempting to rescue crewman from the burning *Clarion*." (*Duluth Evening Herald*)[cxxxi] The *Ashtabula*, a car ferry of the Canadian Pacific Railway that is similar to the No. 2, ran aground near Port Burwell. The crew was well provisioned and able to ride out the storm for a time. The situation began to deteriorate, however. "The fires are out and the boat is fast filling with water. The probabilities are that the men will have to abandon the boat before long. The scene surrounding the big helpless boat is wild in the extreme, waves dashing high over her funnels and sides." (*St. Thomas Daily Times*)[cxxii] Ultimately, the weather subsided sufficiently for the men to be rescued.

In short, a wild and violent gale had descended on both the lake and the coastlines. What had been poor weather as the No. 2 left harbor on Tuesday morning had descended into a full-blown gale by nightfall, with mounting waves, 70 mph winds and blinding snow and ice. Temperatures dropped from 40 degrees Fahrenheit to 10 degrees in a matter of hours. It is reported that visibility at times had dropped to near zero. The barometer dropped to 29.6 as a low-pressure area engulfed the Great Lakes region. The *Marquette & Bessemer No. 1*, photographs of which appear earlier, was a ship of lower profile that left 2 hours earlier and completed its trip across the lake (In one later report it is learned she may have found shelter behind Long Point). The No. 1 was captained by Murdock Rowan who was Captain McLeod's cousin. The No. 2 was not so fortunate. Sailing alone in this maelstrom was the car ferry. "The storm was no little affair, but a storm equal in all respects to the March blizzards of recent years. The storm swept right up from the southwest and left its mark everywhere. The storm greatly affected the big railroads & all of the passenger trains of both the Lakeshore and the Nickel Plate were way behind schedule both yesterday and today. All the wires are out of commission and traffic is being delayed to quite an extent." (*Conneaut News-Herald*)[cxxiii]

The hazards to the car ferry would have been many. The howling winds and snow would have obstructed visibility and made handling the big ship extremely difficult. Boarding seas and spray would steadily ice the boat up and add enough weight to potentially unbalance the ship. Men would have to venture out on to the decks with axes to control the rapidly accumulating hazard. As this was long before the days of radar, navigation would be done by compass and visual landmarks that would likely be obscured in the storm. The winds would be constantly attempting to drive the ship off course. While the Marquette & Bessemer Dock and Navigation Company would mandate wireless radio on its car ferries as a result of the No. 2's loss, the No. 2 had no radio. Its only communication would be its steam whistle, flares, and signal flags. The narrow channels, especially those poorly marked, would be very difficult and hazardous to enter on such conditions, if not impossible.

Ernest McLaren's account of his harrowing experience on the lake is instructive of just how bad this storm was. McLaren was the pilot of the steamer *Jodhua W. Rhodes* which reached Buffalo on Saturday, December 10.th

"Mr. McLaren said this was the worst storm he had seen in his seven years on the lake. When the Jodhua W. Rhodes docked at Buffalo, her decks were covered with six inches of ice. There were only a couple tons of coal left, and this only would have lasted an hour and a half. For sixty hours, we battled for our lives. The steamer was loaded with wheat, and the cargo shifted, causing the boat to list two feet. There was so much ice, that it was impossible to see out the pilot house." (*Evening Free Press*)[cxxiv]

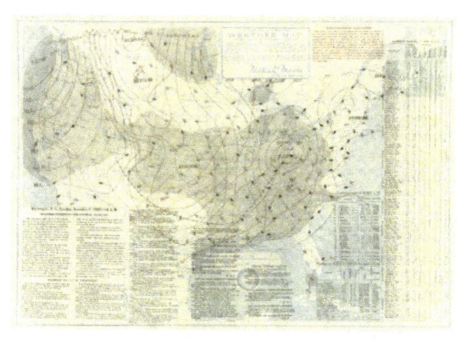

Above is the Department of Agriculture's weather report for Tuesday, December 7,th 1909. It shows a brutal winter storm about hit Lake Erie like a hammer, predominately from the southwest. Document courtesy of the Historical Collections of the Great Lakes, Bowling Green State University.

As the *Marquette & Bessemer No. 2* fought its way through the blizzard, part of the confusion over the fate of the ship is the number of times it was either seen or heard from shore. There were multiple reports of sightings or people hearing the ship's whistle on both sides of the lake. Some of these reports are conflicting, and because of time and distance apart, cannot all be accurate. This further adds to the confusion and mystery in the No. 2's loss.

Our ghost ship was heard more than seen in a myriad of places. I will include here as many of the reports I have been able to locate. I will endeavor to put them in chronological order as much as possible.

"Mr. Wheeler, a Canadian customs officer, stated firmly that he had seen her laboring in mountainous seas and trying to make harbor late Tuesday afternoon, about seven hours after leaving Conneaut. But Captain McLeod, according to Wheeler, was apparently unwilling to chance the narrow entrance with the wind and sea coming from a dangerous angle." (Boyer)[cxxv] This report is very credible and makes sense. The No. 2 probably did make the Canadian coast off Port Stanley. Two hours added to its travel time given the deteriorating weather also makes sense. Captain McLeod was likely

53

not able to navigate the narrow harbor channel in such conditions. Wheeler further reported the ship turned west to seek shelter at Rondeau. This was the first the ship was seen since being sighted by the inbound tug *Alberta T.*

The next report puts the No. 2 on the Ohio side of the lake a mere 3 hours later.

"Mrs. James Holland reported, who lived near Fairview, west of Erie, revealed that she and her son had heard distress signals out on the lake on Tuesday night, only earlier. It was about seven o'clock, she recalled. 'My son, Harold came into the house saying there was a boat in distress almost directly out from us. The sound then stopped, but the distress signal returned about midnight.'" (Boyer)[cxxvi] This puts the car ferry off the Ohio coast around 2 or 3 hours later on Tuesday than it was seen off Port Stanley, at least for the seven o'clock report. As this is a five-hour trip in good weather; both reports cannot be completely accurate. The midnight report is more plausible, however. The next reports are both off the Ohio coast, only later.

"A.H. Brebner says he remembers hearing a whistle early Wednesday morning which sounded at the time like the ferry whistle. Other people heard more or less whistling off Conneaut early Wednesday Morning." (*Erie Times-News*)[cxxvii]

"The master and chief engineer of the steamer Black are confident that the ferry passed them while the Black was lying at anchor just off Conneaut Tuesday night. Both men say they are confident that it was the ferry for the *Marquette & Bessemer No. 2* was like no other boat on Lake Erie and had many features by which a marine man could easily distinguish her." (*Conneaut News-Herald*)[cxxviii]

This report puts the car ferry off Conneaut around midnight on Wednesday. This report also was the source of the rumor that a ship at anchor off the harbor was blocking access, preventing the No. 2 from making Conneaut harbor. This was one of the first pieces of information regarding the car ferry published. It first appeared in the *Conneaut News-Herald* and has been quoted as a factual account in many articles and documents since. It is included in Boyer's 1968 book as well. When I first started working on this book, because the sighting was reported by an officer and engineer on another steamship who should know the No. 2 well, I thought this was one of the most credible reports. If, however, one keeps digging through the microfilm copies of the 100 plus year-old newspaper at the Conneaut Library, one finds that this report was actually retracted in the *Conneaut News-Herald* on December 14th. The retraction reads as follows:

"Like many another story which has gone the rounds during the past few days in connection with the loss of the car ferry, the evidence which pointed to the fact that the boat might have been close to this harbor early Wed morning has dissipated into thin air. The officers & crew of the steamer Black say that it was not they who identify the car ferry as the boat which was whistling off the local port, & Mr. Brebner declines to stand sponsor for any connection with such a supposition. The probabilities are in the opinion of the best informed and particularly among the lake Capts. now at this port, that the boat went down off Long Point & was never near Conneaut after leaving Tuesday Morning." (*Conneaut News-Herald*)[cxxix]

It is also most likely that the steamer *Black* was not even off Conneaut that Tuesday night. Lower water levels at the limekiln crossing delayed several downbound steamers on December 7th, including the Black. (*Cleveland Plain Dealer*)[cxxx]

The *Black* was ultimately logged leaving Detroit, downward bound at 6:40 PM on Tuesday, December 8th. (*Cleveland Plain Dealer*)[cxxxi] Six hours or so does not seem like sufficient time to cover such a large distance between Conneaut and Detroit. Others have postulated it was the *Meachum*, not the Black, that was anchored off Conneaut Harbor, potentially obstructing entrance into the channel. The *Meachum* left at 2:10 PM Tuesday allowing more time to potentially be off Conneaut.(*Cleveland Plain Dealer*)[cxxxii] Interestingly, the *Richardson* is also logged as leaving Detroit downbound at 11:00 AM. (*Cleveland Plain Dealer*)[cxxxii] We will never know for sure if there was a ship moored near the entrance of the harbor obstructing the entrance, or which one it may have been. If Captain McLeod was there that night, it is clear he found the channel too dangerous to enter.

Like many other retractions in newspapers, this one was small and easy to miss. Anyone researching the loss of the car ferry would note the dearth of headlines past a certain point and figure there were no relevant stories. In Mr. Boyer's defense, his was a book about several missing ships, with only one chapter devoted to the No. 2. This was a tiny retraction and easy to miss. We will never know what the source of the original story was. It may have been reported second hand as rumor or scuttlebutt picked up in a harbor bar, not verified, and reported as factual shortly after the sinking.

Mr. Brebner was reported to be a member of the *Alberta T*'s crew and should know the car ferry well. Note that Mr. Brebner's report of hearing the ship's whistle is being reported in the *Erie Times-News* a day after it is being retracted in the *Conneaut News- Herald*. Such is life before the Internet.

Were this the end of it, we could be relatively confident that the No. 2 was not off Conneaut Wednesday morning, although we do have other reports that could be the No. 2 off the coast east of Conneaut. Then there is this report that, unlike that of Mr. Brebner and the officers of the steamer *Black*, was never recanted.

"William Rice, an operator on the Hulett machine (a large mechanized mechanical unloader for those who did not grow up in a Great Lakes port) on Dock One, at the Conneaut harbor reports he was on his machine about 1:30 AM Wednesday, working in an endeavor to keep the machine from freezing. While outside, he heard a boat whistle sound four times, being a distress signal. He said it sounded a short distance northeast of the harbor." (*Conneaut News- Herald*)[cxxxiv] Rice also reported that afterward, he heard the whistle blow "five times, which I thought was the at anchor signal. Pretty soon, as if the anchor chains parted, she started the distress signal again, but in about fifteen minutes, all the blowing stopped." (Boyer)[cxxxv] This is certainly an interesting report as this is an individual who worked around the harbor and should know the ship. Initially, I had some questions as to whether this report made a great deal of sense to me, as it seems the harbor was shutting down. There is plenty of evidence, however, that the end of season deliveries was still continuing. The need for coal was so acute that the Marquette & Bessemer Dock and Navigation Company wasted no time rushing a ship in to replace the No. 2. "Pere Marquette's No. 19 car ferry will take the place of the Bessemer Steamer No. 2 and will reach Port Stanley on Thursday to go into commission between Port Stanley and Conneaut. The immediate provision by the company in shipment of coal from the other side." (*The Evening Free Press*)[cxxxvi] While the car ferry would not use the Hulett equipment, it is likely there were still a few late shipments coming into Conneaut, so it is plausible that William Rice may have been working on the Hulett that Wednesday morning. Keep in mind the sound of a ship's whistle can travel some distance, so the ship may not have been directly off Conneaut Harbor if the report is accurate.

We next have reports of our ghost ship about ten miles to the East of Conneaut. These reports are a little similar, but differ in the details enough, that I think they are two separate reports, not a single incident reported twice.

"Mrs. Adam Large was a resident of North Springfield, an Ohio town about ten miles east of Conneaut. Mrs. Large has often seen the car ferry and knew it by its light. Just before midnight, Tuesday of last week, she went out of door. She remarked on going into the house that she could see the car ferry out in the lake and wondered what it could be doing out there. The family talked about it and went out to see if it really was the car ferry, but they saw no lights. Mrs. Large believes the lights she saw were those of the car ferry, and that the vessel sank while she was in the house." (*Erie Times-News*) cxxxvii Initially, I thought Mrs. Large may be the same women whose story is retold in Boyer's book on page 162 who put the light out to keep the ship from running aground.

In Boyer's account, the car ferry was also seen by a Finnish women Tuesday night east of Conneaut. At first, I thought this might be the same story as Mrs. Adam Large, but they are different enough that I am convinced they are two separate accounts. Additionally, Large does not strike me as a Finnish name.

This second woman was interviewed by Frank Snyder, a local fisherman, and Charles J. McGill, the superintendent of dock operations. "The woman was adamant and would not be shaken from her story. I heard the car-ferry's whistle and knew it well. I saw her lights-white in the middle and red and green to each side, like she was headed back to shore. I quickly put a light in the window and watched as the ship's lights dipped out of sight. The next time only the green light was visible (indicating a sharp turn to port), and then I could only see the tall, white stern light as the ship turned safely back to sea." (Boyer)cxxxviii

This gives us three reports of a ship in trouble early Wednesday morning off the Ohio coast in a fairly tight time frame. In each case, these witnesses seem adamant. It is possible the No. 2 could have made it back to the Ohio coast after being seen off Port Stanley in the afternoon.

Perhaps, it was the *W.C. Richardson*, battered and partially flooded, lumbering up the coast east of Conneaut, heading toward Buffalo, that people saw when they reported lights and a whistle off the Ohio coast. It's not likely in my mind because the *W.C. Richardson* does not appear to have sounded a distress whistle at that time as the ship made it all the way to Buffalo, but perhaps she was visible to some witnesses.

The next report takes us back to Port Stanley only an hour and a half later. This takes us back to Mr. Wheeler, the customs agent at Port Stanley, along with other witnesses.

"At three O'clock on Wednesday morning, Wheeler heard the car-ferry's whistle off the harbor entrance. Two other men, one a schoolteacher, corroborated his story." (Boyer) These reports would put the car ferry off Port Stanley at about 6:00 pm Tuesday and 3:00 AM Wednesday morning.

Obviously while the car ferry could be back around the Ohio coastline at midnight or later Wednesday morning, there is no way the ship could be back off Port Stanley a mere one and a half hours later. One of these reports has to be incorrect.

Wheeler's, however, is not the only report of the car ferry off the Canadian coast early Wednesday morning. "A resident of Port Bruce, about seven miles east of Port Stanley, was awoken about 5:00 AM Wednesday morning by a ship's whistle so close, he thought the vessel had run aground. I could hear her plain as day but couldn't see her because of the snow. Finally, the sound kept getting dimmer, and after a bit, I couldn't hear anything but waves and wind." (Boyer)[cxxl]

"Among those who have stated that they heard the Bessemer's whistle, beyond any doubt, is Capt. Mathew Payne, postmaster at Port Stanley and a former customs officer. It was formerly Mr. Payne's duty to get up to meet the Bessemer each time she came in and from force of habit he hears the whistle every time it blows. He is positive that he heard the whistle on Wednesday morning at about five o'clock, and he believes the vessel was trying to make the harbor." Mr. Farr, the present custom's officer, corroborated hearing the whistle at that time. (*The Evening Free Press*)[cxxli]

"Several residents at Port Stanley said yesterday that at about five o'clock Wednesday morning they heard the distress whistles of a steamer now thought to have been the Bessemer, which would be one to ten miles out in the lake. A heavy northwest gale was blowing." (*St. Thomas Daily Times*) [cxlii]. This gives us an interesting piece of weather information in that on the Canadian side, the weather had shifted, coming out of the northwest early Wednesday morning. Note that the predominate direction of the storm was from the southwest shifting to the west on much of the lake. This information is important as it impacts the drift of wreckage.

If true, the car ferry may have either been in distress, or possibly sounding her whistle in hope of hearing a response from a ship at harbor. In the poor visibility, with blinding snow and accumulating ice, the No. 2 may have not been able to find the channel and may not have been able to pass through safely if it had. One serious challenge to entering any of the small Canadian ports at night in a storm was the apparent lack of proper lighting or signals marking the harbor entrances. One of the few positive outcomes of this story was an inquiry after the wreck brought by Minister of Marine to address this issue. (*London Free Press*)[cxliii]

Photo is courtesy of the Elgin County Archives. It shows the replacement *Marquette & Bessemer No. 2* at Port Stanley, probably sometime after 1910. This picture displays well how narrow the channel is. I do not see much evidence of lighting in this picture, although the view is limited.

These accounts paint a picture of the car ferry desperately seeking shelter or riding the storm out on the lake throughout Tuesday afternoon to early Wednesday or possibly Thursday morning. There were other reports as well.

Donna Isabell McLeod Rodebaugh, niece of both Captain Robert and First Mate John McLeod, spent tremendous time and energy collecting information about the No. 2 and by all accounts was also actively engaged in searching for it. In response to a *Cleveland Plain Dealer* story about the wreck in 1986, Rodebaugh received a letter from Gladys Eagle, aged 93 on November 16, 1986. She reports hearing the whistle of a ship that night about 1.5 miles to 2.0 miles from the PA state line and that she can still hear it vividly in her mind. She vividly recalls thinking the ship sank off the coast. Gladys Eagle's report was not specific about time. (Historical Collection of the Great Lakes)[cxliv]

She was not the only person to hear the ship's whistle on the Ohio side of the lake. What I find interesting is that this is one of the least reported encounters amongst the information I've reviewed. "It was on the Wednesday night before the Marquette and Bessemer No. 2 was given up when one of those women sat up in her home and heard the whistle of the steamer. That woman was Mrs. R.R. McLeod, whose husband was captain of the car ferry. She knew the note of the vessel as well as the tread of her husband's walk." (*Cleveland Plain Dealer*)[cxlv]

Note Mrs. McLeod is quoted as hearing the ship's whistle Wednesday night. I am thinking this is a mistake in the reporting of the story, and the reporter meant to write early Wednesday morning, which better corroborates with the other reports of the car ferry. If it indeed was Wednesday night, that might change the narrative of the story. Putting the car ferry outside Conneaut again on Wednesday night would mean she sank Wednesday night or Thursday morning instead of earlier. Again, this is one of those things we will probably never know for sure. I have not seen Captain McLeod's wife quoted in detail elsewhere, so we may have to take this time at face value.

Were that to be true, that might lend some credence to reports of the ship's whistle off Port Bruce on Thursday as the ship would still have been afloat Wednesday night. This would imply the ship was able to stay afloat for 48 hours past its departure. I still think the No. 2 sank Wednesday morning due to vulnerabilities the ship had which we have already discussed, but it could have been later.

There are now reports of our ghost ship off the Canadian shore on Tuesday afternoon, Wednesday morning and possibly Thursday. So we have our ghost ship off the Ohio coast late Tuesday and early Wednesday morning and possibly later. I'm pretty sure I missed one in there somewhere.

Of course, our ghost ship cannot be off Port Stanley at 3:00 AM Wednesday and off Port Bruce at 5:00 AM if she was off Conneaut at 1:30 AM as Mr. Rice reported. One of these reports has to be partially or mostly incorrect. Of interest, I did discover that an early report of Mr. Wheeler's account that puts the report at 3:00 AM Thursday, not Wednesday. (*Conneaut News-Herald*) This timing makes things much more plausible. If we take the early Wednesday reports of Canada as actually occurring on Thursday morning, everything else does make more sense.

It does put the car ferry as still afloat early Thursday morning if true. If both Rice's report of the ship being off Conneaut at 1:30 AM along with the other residents that saw or heard the No. 2 off the Ohio coast early Wednesday are taken into account along with the report of the resident at Port Bruce hearing the ferry at 5:00 AM Wednesday, then there has to be some type of inaccuracy here. The ship could not get to both places so quickly. Was Mr. Wheeler's 3:00 AM report Thursday morning instead of Wednesday? What about the other reports off the Canadian coast early Wednesday? Are these reports actually early Thursday? This would also make the Wednesday night report by Murdine McLeod fit better. Either Mr. Boyer, The *Conneaut News-Herald*, or other reporting sources have made some type of an error or the report itself is wrong. The complete accurate truth will be lost to history, as at this point, we cannot truly know.

There were other accounts that place the boat on the both the Ohio and Canadian sides of the lake. At this point it is almost impossible to be sure which are completely accurate. There are reasons to believe most of them, except for those that were refuted by the principles themselves, such as the officers of the steamer *Black* or Mr. Brebner. Even with reports I put a great deal of credence in, such as Captain McLeod's wife, who surely would know the sound of her husband's ship, we cannot be sure the time reported is accurate. These reports are sufficiently conflicting, and may be subject to enough reporting errors, that we cannot use them to determine exactly when or where the ship sank.

The reports paint the picture of a boat and captain unable to gain the shelter of harbor because of the weather and other issues. Captain McLeod also may have been playing a delaying game, trying to outlast the horrible weather until he could make harbor. Mr. Wheeler's report of seeing the *Bessemer* Tuesday afternoon, declining to enter the harbor because of treacherous wind and waves seems plausible. It fits the logic of the regular trip from Conneaut to Port Stanley which normally takes 5 hours being delayed by weather and a captain trying to protect his ship and exposed stern using course adjustments. Most of the reports, taken by themselves, seem plausible. It is their incompatibility with each other which makes their veracity a challenge.

Mr. Wheeler's account of the ship heading toward Rondeau would put the No. 2 outside of that harbor in the apex of the storm and she would likely fare no better there. Several schools of thought feel the ship went to Rondeau and then turned south back to the Ohio shore, working its way back up to Conneaut in the lee of the Ohio shore. It makes some intuitive sense in that Captain McLeod would likely try to keep his bow into the storm at that time. Were Captain McLeod to do this, I wonder why he would simply not make a run for Cleveland. I think it is entirely possible that Mr. Wheeler did indeed see the ship turn west, or to port. If the No. 2 was to execute a turn away from Port Stanley, Captain McLeod would have turned to port to avoid exposing his stern to following seas. It is possible what Mr. Wheeler saw was Captain McLeod beginning to execute his turn before making a southerly course back to Conneaut. Some think the ship sank there, trying to execute the turn, or between Port Stanley and Rondeau.

The whistle and sighting reports are muddled at best. They all seem legitimate, but they put the No. 2 on both sides of the lake in time frames so close as to not be possible. This is one of the factors I think has added a great deal of mystery to the story. All of the reports seem sincere, but they can't possibly all be completely correct. Such is the nature of eyewitness testimony. Two of the reports of the No. 2 off Conneaut had been recanted after publication, but there were enough other reports placing the No. 2 or another boat off the coast of Ohio early Wednesday morning to give one pause. Additionally, we really can't be sure of the accuracy of the reporting itself. There is reason to believe some of the dates or times may be incorrectly reported.

If we use some of these times as estimates, it seems highly likely the No. 2 could have been off the Canadian shore early Tuesday afternoon or evening, as well as off the Ohio shore sometime around 1:30 AM as reported by the Hulett operator William Rice, but this would not give the ship sufficient time to be off the Canadian shore sometime around 5:00 AM, much less 3:00 AM. This is especially true given the brutal weather conditions. On Tuesday afternoon, it is reported Captain Murdoch Rowan and the No. 1 took 7 hours to traverse 7 miles during the apex of the storm heading into the wind on his way to Rondeau. (Hibbert)[cxlvii] One of these groups of reports cannot be completely accurate, unless the Canadian reports are really Thursday morning instead of Wednesday, as reported early on in the *Conneaut News-Herald*. Even then, the *News-Herald* report does not account for the report off Port Bruce. It is important to understand that for our purposes, the sighting or hearing of a ship in distress does not necessarily indicate that is where the vessel sank or when. It is merely a clue. Ultimately my writing of this story has three goals; to retell the story of the ship and brave officers and crew, give us a glimpse into the times in which they lived, and ultimately, try to determine the most probable final resting place of the *Marquette & Bessemer No. 2*.

If one finds the Wednesday morning reports of the car ferry being off the Canadian coast credible, then the veracity of the reports of the ship being seen and heard off Ohio really don't impact the location of the sinking. The ship may have been off the coast of Ohio late Tuesday night or early Wednesday morning, but if one accepts subsequent reports off Canada it is unlikely the vessel foundered off Ohio. But we cannot be sure if we look *only* at the reports. If the Captain McLeod's wife truly heard the ship's whistle Wednesday night instead of early Wednesday morning, all that tells us for sure was that the ship was still afloat at that point and where it was at that time. The same is true of the Thursday morning reports of the ship's whistle, though those are undoubtedly closer to the time of the sinking as we have no subsequent reports.

It is still difficult to put tremendous stock in some of the eyewitness accounts. Individuals also may have simply wanted to be part of the story. The car ferry was a well-known vessel, and crew members were popular members of communities on both sides of the lake. It represented a substantial loss. Individuals got inserted into the story in various ways. This may reflect a desire to be part of the story or for other purposes. Conducting the double funeral for Harry Thomas and Roy Hinds (two crewman recovered in lifeboat No. 4 that we will discuss in more detail in the next chapter) Rev E.G. Powel got into print by sharing a vision he had of the loss and Harry Thomas's accension into heaven. The reverend stated the men in the lifeboat were "happy and prepared to meet death and not cringing with fear." (*The Evening Free Press*)[cxlvii] This story was surely of comfort to the family, and Rev. Powel knew Thomas well, but possibly this vision was conjecture. As I read the newspapers of the day, many seemed eager to interject themselves into the story. Loss of the No. 2 was a topic of interest, and many people seemed eager to add their opinions. This is not to say that any of these accounts are meant to be disingenuous, but any courthouse attorney will tell you that human recollection can be a flawed and malleable thing.

A further issue is that in many of these cases we are also talking about reports of the ship's whistle in what is essentially a blizzard. The sound of a ship's whistle can travel ten miles and is affected by wind. Apparently, sound waves can be pushed down toward the ground when traveling into a wind and lifted up from the ground surface with the wind behind it. Because of this dynamic, sound may not be heard evenly or the same way in each location. Direction of a sound is apparently also tricky to measure. This fact was brought home to me recently in a personal way. I do live in an urban neighborhood, and I heard some gunfire recently one night. While not common, this can happen. I reported it as it seemed significant, more so than some idiot just shooting into the sky. I would have bet anything the sound was coming from the southwest. I spoke to a policeman friend the next morning, and he advised me the shooting was actually directly north of me. That was instructive. Perception of sound is not always so straightforward, and personal estimates of direction and distance may be off significantly. My friend tells me such errors are quite common.

Reading these reports makes it difficult to assess with confidence what was going on in Captain McLeod's mind and what he was trying to accomplish. It seems clear he did get to Port Stanley and deemed it far too dangerous to enter. Did he then turn around and try to make Conneaut harbor, being blocked by ships anchored outside the harbor? Did he then try to run up the Ohio coast to Erie, attempting to gain some shelter from the coastline near Presque Isle? Did he attempt to anchor the boat? Some have speculated that once he reached Port Stanley, he may have continued west to try and reach Rondeau or even turned south to Cleveland or another Ohio port, keeping his bow pointed toward the storm. The latter is not supported based on the reports of the ship's whistle or sightings, should we believe them. Had Captain McLeod turned to Rondeau and then to the south, at that point, why wouldn't he have attempted to make harbor at Cleveland, Fairport Harbor or Ashtabula?

The No. 2 may have been feeling her way in the blinding snowstorm, trying to find an answering whistle, or perhaps simply announcing her presence, or her distress. There were no whistles reported off Rondeau. It seems the No. 2 was heard easily enough off Port Stanley, Port Bruce, Conneaut, and east of Conneaut along the Ohio shore. It was reported that Captain Rowan was sent on precisely that course searching for the No. 2 and found no wreckage. (Boyer)[clxix] Had the ship gone down early along that course, Captain Rowan should have encountered this wreckage. It is not to say that the *Marquette & Bessemer No. 2* did not take that course; perhaps it did. What is probable is that she did not sink there. Once again, a very small blurb in the *Conneaut News-Herald* calls this report into question.

"No. 1 did not search for the No. 2. It was falsely reported here that Capt. Rowan had been looking for the lost ferry. The carferry No. 1 (as we have seen, really a collier, not a ferry), which has been at Port Rowan since the heavy storm of Tuesday a week ago, arrived here on Wednesday. The boat took on a cargo and again departed for the other shore. The boat left here on its former trip December 7th. The report was common that the ferry No. 1 was making a search for the missing sister boat. This was not the case and the only searching was done by the tugs that were sent out." (*Conneaut News-Herald*)[clxx]

If we can assume the tugs cast a wide net in the search, and it was thought the boat may have headed toward Rondeau, the premise that wreckage should have been discovered still holds, but is less concrete. This example reinforces how difficult it is to know the facts of our mystery.

It appears the No. 1 went to Port Rowan to shelter behind Long Point (the large peninsula that juts out into Lake Erie), possibly making its delivery to Rondeau much later before returning to Conneaut. This report also calls into question the notion of the No.1 fighting its way through the apex of the storm on its way to Rondeau that was cited previously. Is the report accurate? Is the retraction accurate? Perhaps the story of the crew of the No. 1 battling to get to Rondeau is true, and Captain Rowan gave up, opting for the shelter of Long Point. Perhaps he never attempted Rondeau. Where did the original story come from? Such was reporting of the day. Like the retraction of the crew of the *Black*, the original story is prominently reported and the retraction appears later in a small paragraph with little detail. It is easy to see how such a thing can be reported as fact as the decades roll on.

Did Captain McLeod attempt to reach the shelter of Long Point? Such was the most accepted theory of the day. McLeod, like many lake captains, had sheltered behind Long Point in the past, sometimes for extended periods of time. Many ships took shelter behind Long Point in this storm. If the No.2 was off Port Stanley and Bruce at 5:00 AM Wednesday morning, were they attempting to make harbor, or was the ship merely lost in a blinding snowstorm? Were those reports are really Thursday morning instead of Wednesday as the report in the *Conneaut News-Herald* intimates? Ultimately, we will never know the full details of the ship's last voyage, which reports are accurate, and which aren't. Finding the wreck may give us some partial answers.

Many of the reports of the ship's whistle seem fairly credible, if somewhat contradictory in the details. One can pick and choose those that support their narrative of the events, or dismiss them all, arguing the fallibility of eyewitness testimony. Even if all are accurate, which cannot be, it doesn't exactly tell us where the ship may have gone down. One thing that is evident is that the No. 2 was not definitively heard from after Thursday morning, though these late accounts seem less concrete. It is impossible to tell for sure. While these various reports add to the mystery, terror, and excitement of our story, we cannot rely on them alone to determine what happened to the No. 2. Many of the eyewitness reports actually add, rather than detract from the confusion of the story.

The chart and table on the next page summariz these various reports and attempts to reconcile them with what was probable. More reliable analysis of the physical evidence is required.

Summary of Reported Signals/Sightings of the No. 2. Tuesday Dec. 7-Thursday Dec. 9

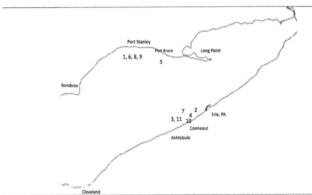

Report Type	Reporter	When	Location	Confidence	Source
1. Sight	Mr. Wheeler	Tuesday Afternoon	Port Stanley ON	High	Boyer
2. Whistles	Mrs. Holland	Tuesday Evening 7 Or Midnight	Fairview PA	Low for 7 Higher for Midnight	*Erie Times-News*
3. Whistle	William Rice	Early Wed. Morning	Near Conneaut	Interesting	Boyer
4. Sight	Mrs. Large	Late Tuesday	N. Springfield PA	Low-Medium	*Erie Times-News*
5. Whistle and Lights	Woman interviewed	Late Tuesday	Ohio	Low-Medium	Boyer
6. Whistle	Mr. Wheeler	3:00 AM Wed. Or 3:00 AM Thursday	Port Stanley	High	Boyer/ *Conneaut News-Herald*
7. Whistle	?	~5:00 AM Wed.	Port Bruce	Medium	Boyer
8. Whistle	Matthew Payne Mr. Farr	~5:00 AM Wed.	Port Stanley	High	*The Evening Free Press*
9. Whistle	Residents	~5:00 AM Wed.	Port Stanley	High	*St. Thomas Daily Times*
10. Whistle	Gladys Eagle	Tuesday Night	PA State Line	Low	Historical Collection of the Great Lakes
11. Whistle	Mrs. McLeod	Wed. Night or Wed. Morning	Near Conneaut	Medium	*Cleveland Plain Dealer*

Note: The schematic of the chart and table show the cluster of reports over three days. Two other reports were given off Conneaut — one of a sighting reported in Boyer and another of a distress whistle reported in the *Conneaut News-Herald* — were both later retracted. We discount them here.

Chapter Five: The Lifeboat

It was 10:00 AM Sunday morning, December 12th, when the state fishing tug *Commodore Perry* met the grisly sight of the battered half sunken yawl boat with its frozen cargo of nine dead men and the clothing of a likely tenth occupant 15 miles northwest of Erie, PA. The crew of the Perry, fearing the boat would capsize if they attempted to board it, opted to tow it into Erie, Pa. This yawl was the No. 4 lifeboat of the *Marquette & Bessemer No. 2*, and its dark cargo removed all speculation about the fate of the ship. The nine frozen crewmen aboard the battered boat were taken to the morgue in Erie, PA and subsequently identified as:

- Thomas Steele, Fireman, aged 24 years.

- Joseph Shank, Fireman, aged approximately 25 years.

- Charles Allen, Coal passer, aged approximately 18 years.

- George Smith, Steward, aged approximately 33 years.

- William Ray, Oiler, aged 25 years.

- John "Paddy" Hart, Oiler, aged approximately 38 years.

- Harry Thomas, Second cook, aged 22 years.

- R. Hines, Coal passer, age unknown.

- J.W. (Manny) Souars (Soares), Waiter, aged 20.

I have seen a staggering array of spellings for J.W. Soares. I will use Soares, which is the spelling listed on his Pennsylvania death certificate. (Historical Collection of the Great Lakes)[cli] Roy Hinds's body was originally identified as O'Hagan, but a Port Stanley clergyman identified Hines. (*London Free Press*)[clii]

Lifeboat No. 4. Photo courtesy of the Historical Collections of the Great Lakes, Bowling Green State University.

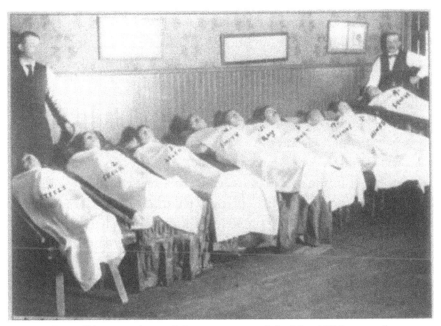

The well-known photo of the occupants of the No. 4 lifeboat at the
Erie, PA morgue.
Photo courtesy of the Historical Collections of the Great Lakes, Bowling Green
State University.

68

There is evidence a tenth man was on board the lifeboat. A set of neatly folded clothing was found frozen to the planking of the lifeboat. As alluded to earlier, this may be O.T.W. Lander, who has appeared on some crew lists. It is his name that appears on an IOU with a five-dollar bill accompanying the clothing frozen to the bottom of the lifeboat. It is likely he had gone mad with despair, neatly folding his clothing on the bottom of the boat and jumping into the freezing lake. (*The Cleveland Plain Dealer*)[cliii] Captain Driscol reported "Eight of the men were sitting upright in the boat, their life preservers strapped about their shoulders. The ninth man lay in the bottom of the boat, frozen to the plank flooring. The faces of the men were bloated. Their clothes heavy with frozen water." (*St. Thomas Daily Times*)[cliv] "All of the rowlocks were shipped, showing that a desperate struggle for life had been made amid the tossing waves and blinding snowstorm before the oars had been swept away from numbed and nerveless fingers." (*Conneaut News-Herald*)[clv]

There have been several accounts of some of the lifeboat occupants huddled over the smallest and weakest crew member to preserve his warmth. This has been reported to be Manny Soares, widely regarded as one of the most popular members of the crew, but also Joseph Shank (spelled Shenk in some accounts). The *Conneaut News Herald* reports some bodies were sitting upright, but huddled in the bottom of the boat to lend warmth to Soares. Captain Driscoll's firsthand account does not make it clear this is the case. It is possible some dramatic license was taken with this part of the tale when it was reported in the papers.

Note that despite a dozen fishing tugs searching the lake for three days, the discovery of the lifeboat was the first absolute evidence the No. 2 had been lost. (*Cleveland Plain Dealer*)[clvi] Many such small, rugged tugs ventured out in horrific weather, returning coated in ice, without success. A good example of such craft included the *Alva B* which participated in the search. The *Alva B* is likely of similar construction to the state fishing tug *Perry* that discovered lifeboat No. 4, as well as other tugs of the time such as the *Alberta T.*, which was the last vessel to see the No. 2 as she was departing Conneaut.

"According to Captain Driscoll (of the *Commodore Perry*) it must have been the last one launched, as Captain McLeod of the ill-fated craft, would have started his boats in the order of their numbers." (*Erie Times-News*) The lifeboat itself was badly battered, suggesting it may have been damaged in its launching, "half filled with water and ice." (*The Cleveland Plain Dealer*)[clvii]

"Only one oar remained with the No. 4 lifeboat, still frozen in the hands of one of the crewmen." (Boyer)

There is considerable evidence that the lifeboat was launched in great haste. "Thomas, the cook, was the only who had worn an overcoat. The (other) eight bodies were dressed in overalls and jumpers, indicating their departure from the car ferry had been hurried. All wore life preservers." (*St. Thomas Daily Times*)

The *Alva. B.*, One of the boats that searched for the No. 2. Photo Courtesy of the Historical Collection of the Great Lakes, Bowling Green State University.

The lack of proper clothing is not the only evidence that the boat was launched in chaos. One is that the boat was only at half capacity. Secondly, there were no officers amongst the crew of the No. 4 lifeboat. "Tradition would dictate that Second Mate Frank Stone would command one of the boats, First Mate John McLeod another, and Captain McLeod, the last boat to leave the ship." (Boyer)[clviii] It is safe to assume Engineer Eugene Wood would have also commanded one of the lifeboats as well. Additionally, lifeboat No. 4 was in very poor condition. It may have been damaged in launching, possibly due to a list the ship had taken on. Another oddity with this hastily launched lifeboat was that Steward George Smith had brought two long galley knives and a meat cleaver with him on the lifeboat. (Boyer)[clix]

70

According to the *Conneaut News-Herald* "The lifeboat occupants were poorly dressed but also poorly provisioned, though they did have a flask of whiskey with them, though they did all have life preservers on (these may have donned these earlier)." The paper goes on to report that this group of the crew "would be the least likely to weather exposure and the high seas and that they were grouped together further gave bore aide to the theory that there had been haste or panic. In addition, the men found were off watch Wednesday morning from midnight 'till six and it is possible the that the others were working down in the hold and they never left there." (*Conneaut News-Herald*)^{clxiii}

I believe that the No. 4 lifeboat was probably launched in haste and without orders. I do believe the No. 4 lifeboat was launched in an act of desperation and fear. I do not blame the lifeboat crew for this if true; after all the ship did sink. I also think the lifeboat was launched close to when the ship sank, probably Wednesday morning, after 5:00AM if we put any credence in the reports of whistles off Port Bruce and Port Stanley early Wednesday morning.

Much was made of the knives and meat cleaver in the lifeboat and the hasty launch in Boyer's book because when Captain Robert McLeod's body was recovered a year later, it was reported there were gash wounds on it. One theory Boyer speculated was that perhaps there was an altercation between the captain and crew when the boat was launched. While I have no evidence to back up my own personal opinion, and there is a great deal of evidence to support the idea that lifeboat No. 4 was launched in great haste, I do not think there was a fight amongst the crew and officers. Is it possible the lifeboat was launched early? I now think that is probable, even likely. It would not be the only lifeboat to leave a ship in distress while it was still afloat.

We can see that in both the *Clarion* and *Richardson* cases; crew and in some cases, officers, took to the lifeboats while the ship was still afloat. I do not believe, however, that Captain McLeod would have left the bridge to confront his men in a time of such crises. This is supported in the account of a former crewman, Fireman Archie Nicholson, of the *Shenango*, who does not believe Captain McLeod would have left the bridge. "Cap McLeod was the kind of officer who would have stayed with his ship," Nicholson declared ith feeling. "Whenever there was rough weather, he was always on the bridge, and I never saw him leave the bridge until the danger had passed. ery man on the boat thought a great deal of him. He was the same to a deckhand as he

71

was to the chief engineer." (*The Evening Free Press*)[clxiv] More likely, these crewmen were just trying to escape the sinking or distressed ship. Knives and a cleaver would have been among the steward's most prized possessions and may have been brought simply for that reason. These would also be useful items for dealing with tangled lines and also to chip away at accumulated ice. After being in Lake Erie for a year, Captain McLeod's body could have come by those wounds in a myriad of ways, including ship's propellers and pack ice.

While the No. 4 lifeboat is the best-known part of the story and clearly the center of great human drama, this was not the only lifeboat recovered. The No. 2 lifeboat from the *Marquette & Bessemer No. 2* was found, empty, about 8 miles East of Port Burwell. "Farmers living eight miles east of this village found one of the lifeboats of the ill-fated Bessemer and a quantity of wreckage on the shore below their farms this morning. The boat was one of the yawl types with air compartments and was marked Marquette and Bessemer." There were no bodies in the boat. (*The Evening Free Press*)[clxv] Of the four main lifeboats, this was the only other intact lifeboat found. "Port Stanley, December 11th, 4:15 PM The tug Winner, of Port Burwell, has just arrived here to coal up, and brings news that a green yawl boat, with three men in it, had been found ashore at Clear Creek, which is located about half way between Port Burwell and Long Point, where wreckage was seen by the W.B. Davock on its way to Detroit." (*St. Thomas Daily Times*)[clxvi] This story may have given rise to reports in some circles that a party of men launched the boat to get help when the No. 2 was relatively close to shore. This story was later however repudiated. "The story that the tug Winner had seen a yawl boat containing three bodies at the mouth of Clear Creek has been investigated and found to be false. There is also no truth in the yarn that a yawl boat had been seen empty. The later rumor probably arose from the fact that the Playfair saw some wreckage from the Clarion." (*St Thomas Daily Times*)[clxvii]

This passage is a little confusing in that it implies a yawl boat was not found at all. On the same page of the same newspaper, it confirms a yawl boat was indeed located east of Port Stanley, undoubtedly our lifeboat No. 2. It further goes on to assess the possibility of the *Marquette & Bessemer No. 2* foundering off Port Stanley Wednesday morning because of the many reports of the ship's whistle at that time. "While it is possible the Bessemer came within hailing distance of the Port at that time, it is considered unlikely by those that have studied the conditions she foundered in, the direction in which her whistle was apparently heard. The wind and currents were so strong that had the Bessemer foundered off Port Stanley, the yawl boats would have been driven far east of where one was found yesterday." (*St Thomas Daily Times*)[clxviii]

While the reports are a little muddled, this apparently was the only other intact lifeboat found from the *Marquette & Bessemer No. 2* This also must be the lifeboat Boyer refers to in his book as well as several other accounts. "Near Port Burwell, one of the lifeboats was found almost intact, and in the flotsam around it, twelve oars. The paint on the oarlocks being unmarked, it was concluded that the boat had not been launched from the ship and broken free because of the air pressure in its floatation chambers." (Boyer) [clxix] Of course, there are reports that differ somewhat in that this report specifically mentions the lack of oars. "Port Burwell, 3:40 PM, Tuesday, another lifeboat belonging to the car ferry Bessemer No. 2 has been picked up about nine miles east of here. The boat was empty and partially filled with water. No oars were found on board. No further bodies have been recovered. Masses of wreckage, undoubtedly from the Bessemer, are continually drifting ashore." (*Saint Thomas Daily Times*)[clxx] Regardless, this has to be the same lifeboat, and it appears it is a safe assumption that the original report from the tug *Winner* is incorrect and that the boat was likely never manned. "The air tanks of a third boat were found nearby, and the broken wreckage of the last lifeboat was found impaled on the rocks at Buffalo Harbor four months later." (Boyer)[clxxi]

What is apparant in the many reports on lifeboat No. 2 found off Port Burwell, whether with or without oars, it appears to have never been launched or occupied. The most definitive statement on this probably came from the Marquette & Bessemer Dock and Navigation company itself "A dispatch from the Walkerville Offices of the company that the yawl boat was found on the Canadian shore, 8 miles east of Port Burwell. There were no bodies in the boat nor was there anything in the boat to indicate it had carried any of the lost men." (*The Conneaut News-Herald*)[clxxii] The rare photo below confirms recovery of the No. 2 lifeboat. This is a photo I have never seen published anywhere, showing the lifeboat on a rail car about to be returned to the Marquette & Bessemer Dock and Navigation Company. This boat appears to be in much better condition than the No. 4 lifeboat recovered in a near broken condition.

The lifeboat No. 2, courtesy of the Elgin County Archive.

It is highly probable that these other three lifeboats or their remains broke free from the ship after it sank and were probably never actively launched by the crew. We will never know with absolute certainty. Conflicting reports like those from the tug *Winner* add to the mystery of the No. 2. The preponderance of evidence indicates, however, that these boats, including the No. 2 lifeboat, were never manned and three frozen bodies were never recovered off Clear Creek.

As evidenced earlier, the No. 2 could not have sunk off Port Stanley because the wreckage would have been driven much further east by the winds and currents. In reality, it is exactly what happened, with one lifeboat being found as far east as Erie, PA. If Boyer is right and the lifeboat No. 2 and the other wreckage broke free from the *Marquette & Bessemer No. 2* after she sank, that could account for it position south to southeast of Port Stanley.

With regard to lifeboat No. 4, we will never know the true conditions under which it was launched, but the evidence points to very dire circumstances. I believe the lifeboat was launched in a time frame that is relatively close to when the ship sank, as I have stated earlier.

In addition to the lifeboats 1 through 4, most of which were wooden (the photo of lifeboat No. 2 clearly shows metallic construction), there appears to be at least one (probably more) metallic green yawl boats with which the *Marquette & Bessemer No. 2* was equipped, which may have been stowed on the cabin roof or deck. (*The Cleveland Plain Dealer*)[clxxii] Other than their appearance, floating and empty, with other wreckage, I have not seen any other mention of them. It does not appear any were successfully launched.

I think this fact is important because it offers our first important clue in narrowing down the location of the *Marquette & Bessemer No. 2*. Over the decades, there has been speculation that the reason the No. 2 has never been found is because it lies in the deepest water in Lake Erie. The Rodebaughs even launched an expedition to a potential target in deep water. (*The Cleveland Plain Dealer*)[clxxiii] These depths lie mostly beyond Long Point. The weather patterns, the wreckage that mostly wound up on the Ontario shore, and the lifeboat itself tells us this cannot be true. Regardless of the day it sank in the range of December 7th to December 9th, or its exact location, the No. 2's wreckage and its lifeboat would have been subjected to wind from the west, southwest or northwest based on all the weather reports we have. We can assume with relative certitude that the location of the sinking must be west of the lifeboat No. 4, which was found 15 miles due north of Erie, Pennsylvania, and we can eliminate all locations east of the lifeboat, which would include the deepest parts of Lake Erie. Some newspaper articles of the day plot the lifeboat 15 miles northwest of Erie PA. For our purposes, I will use due north, which is a little more conservative when being used to consider eliminating the section of Lake Erie east of the lifeboat. Further, we have to ask ourselves, given the prevailing weather patterns, could the wreck of the *Marquette & Bessemer* be east of the No. 2 lifeboat? Because it was found early with all the other wreckage, and because the winds were out of the west, whether from the southwest or northwest, can the wreck be east of the No. 2 lifeboat found between 8 and 12 miles east of Port Burwell? Probably not.

Was the lifeboat No. 4 launched early by panicked and frightened crew members? I think it is likely. Crew members of the *Richardson* left the boat well before its sinking during this storm. I would not call the launching of the lifeboat on the *Clarion* as unjustified as the ship was actually on fire at the time. Really, none of these crewmen can be second-guessed. The conditions were brutal and terrifying. It is also possible Captain McLeod released his reserve crew with his blessing; we will never know. Regardless, the No. 4 lifeboat was at half capacity, badly damaged, and without officers. As reported earlier, it also appears to be launched out of sequence with what a normal abandon ship order would look like. Still, everything about the dress off the crew and condition of the lifeboat crew suggests the boat was launched in great haste and may have actually been damaged in its launching. I believe the lifeboat was launched very close to or at the time of the sinking. The wind and waves may have carried it a great distance from where the *Marquette & Bessemer No. 2* went down, but I do not believe the wreck can be east of the lifeboat. Therefore, the No. 2 cannot be hiding in the deepest parts of the lake. Had the *Marquette & Bessemer No. 2* made it to that area beyond Long Point, they probably would have survived. And if not, the vast majority of wreckage would not have washed up on Long Point, but beyond it.

The No. 2 lifeboat is an important indicator of where the ship sank. That the No. 2 lifeboat and attendant wreckage were found between 8 and and 12 miles east of Port Burwell, depending on the account, provides us with other clues about the ship's location. It is unclear whether this is part of the large debris field first encountered by the *Davock* on December 10th, or a separate debris field. Regardless, with prevailing winds out of the west, mostly of gale force, it seems unlikely the *Marquette & Bessemer No. 2* would have sunk east of Port Burwell, thus eliminating large stretches of lake.

Regardless of sightings, the ship's whistle or other subjective reports, the weather and the ending location of the wreckage offer evidence that the ship sank further to the west and the north. Due west winds on December 10th and 11th and southwest winds on December 9th would most likely have carried the bulk of the wreckage further east if the No. 2 went down in front of Long Point or off Erie.

Chapter Six: Those That Came Home

We know some things about the fate of the crew on the No. 4 lifeboat. "Hundreds gathered at the dock and awaited the arrival of the *Perry*, with her flag at half-mast and the dead in tow." (*Erie Times-News*)[clxxv] "It is reported that the burial of the bodies recovered will be paid for by the car ferry company. The nine bodies of the sailor men were shipped to Conneaut today, accompanied by over 100 mourners." (*Grand Rapids Press*)[clxxvi]

The loss was grievous to Conneaut, Ohio as so many of the crew were either from Conneaut or kept homes there. "In keeping with the rest of Conneaut's bodies which have postponed any and all affairs a few days in order to show respect for the dead the council last night did likewise." (*Conneaut News Herald*)[clxxvii]

Harry Thomas was ultimately returned to Port Stanley where his funeral was jointly conducted for him and fellow Port Stanley crew member Roy Hines. This was the service in which Reverend E.G. Powell presided. Harry Thomas is buried at the Union United Church Cemetery in Union, Ontario. It is reported he has a grave marker, and Roy Hines's grave is not marked. There have been some conflicting reports, but it seems clear Hines was indeed recovered in the No. 4 lifeboat. There are some variations on the spelling of his name and it appears as Hinds in some reports. (Historical Collection of the Great Lakes)[clxviii]

Charles Allen was returned to his native Pennsylvania. He is buried at North Bend Cemetery in North Bend, Pennsylvania. It is reported he has a marker. (Historical Collection of the Great Lakes)[clxix]

William Ray was returned to his hometown of Butler, Pennsylvania where he was reported to be buried at the South Side Cemetery. (*Butler Citizen*)[clxx]

John "Paddy" Hart and shipmate Joseph Shenk are buried in adjacent plots in the Trinity Cemetery in Erie, Pennsylvania. The graves are reported to be unmarked. (Historical Collection of the Great Lakes)[clxxi]

George Smith is buried in the City Cemetery in Conneaut, Ohio, which is the same cemetery his captain is buried in. He is reported to have a headstone. (Historical Collection of the Great Lakes)[clxxii]

John W. Soares, also referred to at times as Manny, has several different spellings presented in various articles. He is buried at St. Joseph's cemetery in Conneaut, Ohio. (Historical Collection of the Great Lakes)[clxxiii]

The loss of the *Marquette & Bessemer No. 2* had a terrible impact on many in Conneaut and elsewhere. "Nine Hundred Conneaut Citizens crowded into the new high school building's 750 seat auditorium for memorial services for the vanished ship and her lost people, nineteen of them friends and neighbors. Most families had lost their breadwinners. Several were almost destitute. The Elks will attend to these cases as long as their funds hold out. The newspaper itself organized a relief fund, announcing, the first day yielding only twelve dollars. The Gem theatre sponsored a benefit matinee for the relief of widows, turning over its receipts to the newspaper's fund. When the drive closed the day before Christmas, the total was only a modest $1018.00." (Boyer)[clxxiv]

Some of the rest of the crew of the *Marquette & Bessemer No. 2* would slowly find their way home, though they waited until springtime, spending the winter in a suspended animation of pack ice. Some would be found months later, some more than a year later. Some of the bodies were in a horrific condition and undoubtedly could not be identified. A great number of the crew and the one or two passengers on the ship were never recovered and are probably still entombed in the wreck.

May 2nd, Port Colborne "Saturday, R Scott, a farmer living about a mile east of here, on the lake shore road, discovered the body of a man floating near the shore. When the body was brought in, it was found to be one of the men of the ill-fated Bessemer and Marquette car ferry (name reversed in the paper) which foundered in Lake Erie last fall. One of the ferry's life preservers was still on the body. The man's watch and several articles were still in the pockets and from these the body was identified as that of Gene Wood of Conneaut, the engineer of the car ferry." (*Buffalo Evening News*)[clxxv]

"The body was in an advanced state of decomposition. The sisters of Engineer Wood were summoned from Port Dalhousie and positively identified the body. Information was at once given to Mrs. Wood, widow of the engineer and to C.J. McGill at the harbor. Owning to the condition of the body it is thought advisable to have the funeral and burial at Port Dalhousie, Ont., the former home of the engineer, and where he was born and raised (Port Dalhousie is located in St. Catherine's, Ontario). The funeral will be held on Monday. Mrs. Wood leaves this afternoon for Port Colborne by way of Buffalo." (*Conneaut News-Herald*)[clxxvi]

Unlike his brother George, captain of the steamer *Bannockburn*, which is still missing, Engineer Wood made it home. Eugene Wood is buried in St. John's Cemetery in St. Catherine's, Ontario. It is reported he has a grave marker. (Historical Collection of the Great Lakes)[clxxvi]

"Conneaut Ohio, Oct 10th, another body, thought to be off the ferry *Marquette & Bessemer No. 2*, was picked up on the beach at Long Point. From the description, the body appears to be that of William Wilson. A watch that was found on the body has the name of a firm in Lindsay on the face of it. Lindsay was William's home." (*The Cleveland Plain Dealer*)[clxxvii] This was the seventeen-jewel Waltham watch that was his pride and joy that Boyer described. "Lighthouse keeper S. B. Cook made a rough coffin and buried the No. 2's wheelman there on the point where he still sleeps away his personal eternity." (Boyer)[clxxviii] William was found not far from his captain, finally reaching the refuge he was seeking in life.

"The body of Captain John McLeod (First Mate of the No. 2) and older brother of Captain R.R. McLeod, was found in a water intake for the Niagara Falls Power Company. The badly battered and decomposed body of the No. 2' s First Mate was thought to have traveled over 100 miles from the wreck site, under and through the ice, but the clothing was intact. In the pockets were found $125.00 and a bundle of documents. One of the car ferry's lifebelts was attached to the body. Positive identification was made by the personal papers found with the body." (*The Evening Free Press*)[cxc]

"John McLeod had his captains' papers with him and money orders that confirmed his identity. He was still wearing his silver watch, which had stopped at 12:25. He was not wearing shoes, but otherwise, the body was in surprisingly good condition." (*Buffalo Evening News*)[cxci] Note that in the *Buffalo Evening News* story, the body is described as in good condition, versus the *Evening Free Press* report. John McLeod is buried in the Our Lady of Mercy Cemetery, Sarnia, Ontario. There is reported to be a headstone. (Historical Collection of the Great Lakes)[cxcii]

"The second body of the crew of the Bessemer car ferry No. 2, which was lost last December, to be found, has been identified as that of Patrick Keith, coal passer on the steamer. The body was found about three miles off Port Colborne, Ontario. It was identified by a large scar over the right eye and a life preserver on the body which bore the words 'Bessemer, No. 2.' Keith was quite well known here and began work on the car ferry only a month before the disaster." (*Erie Times-News*)[cxciii] Keith was another crew member who was relatively new to the ship. As stated earlier, it is unclear how much experience he had as a sailor.

"Frightfully decomposed body on beach at Harts Farm above Waldameer today. Identification probably impossible. The body of a man believed to be one of the victims of the ill-fated car ferry Marquette & Bessemer No. 2 was found on the beach at Hart's Farm above Waldameer by campers. The body was frightfully decomposed and from appearances had been in the water a long time. Coroner Hanley believes the floater to be one of the wreck victims. The remains will be sent to the poor house and interred without delay. The body was clothed only in porous knit underwear and there were no marks by which the body could be identified. The body's features were entirely obliterated." (*Erie-Times News*)[cxciv] That the man could not be identified and met an anonymous end is a troubling fate to which no one should be subjected. Unfortunately, we will never know this man's identity, or if he was even for sure a member of the No. 2's crew.

"The fish tug Cisco brought in today the body of a man which it had picked up far out in the lake. The body is unrecognizable, but it is thought, because of some of the clothing worn, it is one of the victims of the disaster in which the car ferry *Marquette & Bessemer No. 2* was lost last winter." (*Cleveland Plain Dealer*)[cxcv] Here is another anonymous victim of the terrible 1909 storm and displays why the number of people recovered from the No. 2 will always be an estimate at best.

"The trunk and head of a man believed to be one of the ill-fated car ferry Marquette & Bessemer No. 2 was picked up on Long Point Canada by the tug Shaffer." (*The Cleveland Plain Dealer*)[cxcvi] Here it appears the currents have brought another body to rest at Long Point. In this particular case, I do not think the victim was identified. It is also possible the body is from another of the wrecks in that storm, but based on the sheer quantity of wreckage that arrived on the beaches of Long Point, this is probably one of the No. 2's officers or crew.

"Men, patrolling the beach at Long Point opposite of this city, on Wednesday, discovered a body that had been washed ashore. It is badly decomposed, but the word McLeod tattooed leads to the belief that the remains are those of the captain of the Marquette & Bessemer No. 2, which sank last December with all on board. A dispatch was immediately sent to the widow of Captain McLeod in Cleveland, informing her of the finding of the body." (*Erie Times-News*)[cxcvii]

Special to the *Plain Dealer*, Ashtabula, Oct 6- "The body of Capt. R.R. McLeod, master of the car-ferry Marquette & Bessemer No. 2, which was lost last December, was recovered at Long Point Wednesday and positively identified by the name tattooed on one arm." (*The Cleveland Plain Dealer*)[cxcviii]

This report indicates Captain McLeod was found on October 5th. Boyer reports "It was October 6th when they found the captain. Curiously enough, it was the fifth anniversary of the day he had taken his vessel out on her maiden voyage. It was also the day her replacement, the second *Marquette & Bessemer No. 2* left Conneaut for Port Stanley on her first trip." (Boyer)[cxcix] Either way, close enough.

It is difficult to tell exactly how many were recovered specifically from the *Marquette & Bessemer No. 2*. It appears 14 were positively identified, and 3 or 4 more may have been recovered. This list cannot be a definitive, as there may be other records I have not located. Each of these subtopics could potentially be explored further, but that is beyond the scope and purpose of the book.

Most estimates put the recovered bodies at around 18, of which a list 14 have been identified. In truth, we cannot definitively say how many men were actually on the ship for certain to begin with, but I put it at 32 crew and officers and two passengers. Were passenger Crist Johnson and crewman O.T.W. Lander on the boat? Probably. Was J. O'Hagen on the boat, or was he at a union hall in Cleveland as reported in one account? We don't really know for sure. Was there another crewman recruited at the last minute for this final trip that we don't know about? Possibly. The unknowns in this mystery are great, and dissecting them more than 110 years after the fact requires that we accept there are things about this story we will never know for sure.

One thing we can believe with relative certitude was that passenger Albert Weis was not among the dead recovered. "Mr. Weis's brother reported Albert Weis had distinctive dental work that included bold caps on his teeth." (*Erie Times News*)[cc] None of the bodies recovered had such dental work. Not all of them were identifiable, and its possible some of the bodies recovered above were from other wrecks. One other thing that is safe to assume is that at least a portion of the crew is still entombed in the hulk of the No. 2, resting quietly and undisturbed in their hidden underwater grave for over a century.

Chapter Seven: Flotsam, Jetsam & Rumors

We can see that right after the sinking, as well as decades later, our ghost ship is everywhere, and yet nowhere to be found. The length of time the No. 2 has been missing, the myriad of sightings, some conflicting and confusing, the physical evidence (much of it all over the lake), and relentless yet unproven rumors of the ship's discovery have fed confusion about the wreck's location. Here we will recount the most salient information, much of it at the time of the sinking, and some of it is decades after the fact. Most of this is recounted in newspaper accounts of the day. It is, in some ways, almost too much information.

After the Disaster

The first report I can find of wreckage of the car ferry being encountered was a wireless message from the *W.B. Davock*, encountering wreckage off Long Point. This report appeared in the *Erie Times-News* on Friday, December 10th. The report is littered with errors, including calling the car ferry the *Conneaut* (it was sometimes referred to as the Conneaut car ferry) and misidentifying the number of crew. It was clearly hastily composed, but they could be only talking about the No. 2. (*Erie-Times News*)[cci] In another irony, the *W.B. Davock* would later be lost with all hands while sailing Lake Michigan in the brutal Armistice Day Storm of 1940.

A subsequent corroborating report appeared in the *Plain Dealer* the next day. "The officials of the Marquette & Bessemer Dock and Navigation Company have given up all hope for the car ferry, which is now more than 80 hours overdue. The *W.B. Davock* passed through wreckage in the lower end of Lake Erie yesterday that the owners are convinced is from her. The Davock has been running through light wreckage for about 15 miles above Long Point. Abreast of Long Point, we passed a metallic yawl boat painted green and full of water. We could not make out the name. The *Marquette & Bessemer No. 2* carried a metallic lifeboat." (*The Cleveland Plain Dealer*)[ccii]

Following is another description of the first encounter with wreckage of the No. 2. "It is about 7:00 AM on Friday, December 10, amongst the ice, the W.B. Davock spots a huge debris field after heading up the lake toward Detroit. Debris including the white and green woodwork familiar to the M&B No. 2, life jackets, ship's utensils, life rings and an empty lifeboat seen close to the beach near the end of long point." (*The Lake Erie Beacon*)[ccii] This is undoubtedly the metallic yawl boat mentioned previously and the wreckage is undoubtedly from the *Marquette & Bessemer No. 2*. Several other reports corroborate the *W.B. Davock* encountering this debris field, and it is the first true confirmation, some three days later, that the No. 2 was not merely sheltering out the storm somewhere, but that she was indeed gone.

Some argue that the *Davock* was actually downbound from Detroit and not upbound when she encountered the wreckage off Long Point. This argument is based at least partially due to the *W.B. Davock* having been listed as downbound from Detroit on December 9th at 2:15 PM. (*Cleveland Plain Dealer*)[cciv]. I'm uncertain this is proof the *W.B. Davock* still didn't have time to complete its shipment and begin its return trip, though this seems unlikely. This would have put her traveling continuously instead of sheltering during the worst of the storm and time still may not have been sufficient. What is important for our purposes, whether the ship was upbound or downbound, was that the ship encountered the wreckage off Long Point. This is not in dispute, and that the wreckage is consistent with the *Marquette & Bessemer No. 2*.

The next reports, although some of the most convoluted and confusing in our story, describe the wreckage of the ship's No.2 lifeboat and the air tanks of a third lifeboat 8 to 12 miles east of Port Burrell. These sightings are addressed in the chapter on the lifeboats. The early appearance of this wreckage here is very important to deducing the most probable location of our ghost ship. If the ship went down off the Ohio coast on Dec 8, 9 or 10, with a period of very strong winds from the west, how did a lifeboat and wreckage find its way this far west and north? You can make a case that the debris field was pushed towards Long Point by southwesterly winds if the ship sank between Conneaut and Erie, but this lifeboat and wreckage, discovered early in the process, are almost 30 miles west of the debris field the *W.B. Davock* encountered of Long Point. That discovery makes such a scenario very unlikely. It is possible that the No. 2 sank west of Conneaut and the southwesterly winds drove all the debris to the Canadian shore. While possible, as I will discuss later in the subsequent chapter, why I think this is also unlikely. I believe the wreck is west of where the ship's No. 2 lifeboat was found.

While we cannot be absolutely certain of the surface conditions on the lake at all times, the prevailing winds were very much out of the south to southwest on the Ohio side of the lake with a mix of northwesterly winds coming out of Port Stanley, possibly as early as December 8th. I believe that his lifeboat and wreckage east of Port Burwell strongly suggests that the

Marquette & Bessemer No. 2 could not have foundered off the Ohio coast, or really anywhere between Ashtabula and Erie. The wreckage off Long Point could have been pushed further north off Ohio by southwest winds, but this lifeboat and wreckage? It is too far north and west to have been driven from that point on the Ohio coast. A sustained wind out of the south would have been required, and there is simply no indication of that prior to the finding of the wreckage.

If Boyer's theory is correct and the ship's No. 2 lifeboat broke free from the ship after her sinking, probably on the night of December 8th or the morning of December 9th, this wreckage may be closer to the site of the sinking than the other debris encountered. Had the No. 2 lifeboat broken free from the wreck on say, December 10,[th] it may have been driven directly east from the wreck to where it is was found east of Port Burwell. What we don't know is are we looking at one large debris field running from Long Point to Port Burwell, or two separate fields impacted by different wind conditions. We can never determine this for certain, but I am inclined to think this is two separate debris fields, originating on different days and impacted by different wind conditions.

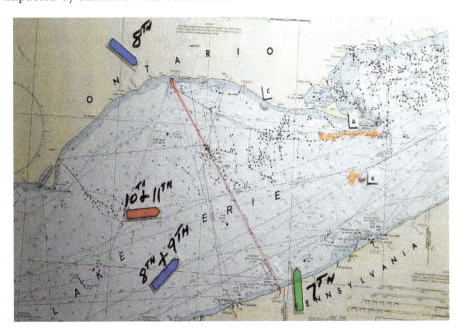

Chart marking the debris field, lifeboat location and wreckage right after the sinking.

In the debris field chart the letter "A" represents the debris field encountered by the *Davock* off Long Point (the large, sandy spit protruding into the lake in the northeast corner of the map), "B" represents the finding of the No. 4 lifeboat 15 miles north of Erie (some wreckage accompanied the lifeboat), and "C" represents the finding of the ship's No. 2 lifeboat. The colored arrows represent wind direction and the dates, December 7th through 11th. The red line marks the course between Conneaut and Port Stanley.

As seen , we have the wreckage encountered by the *Davock*, the No. 4 lifeboat with its frozen crew, and the ship's No. 2 lifeboat located in quick succession, with prevailing winds out of the southwest, west and northwest. The colored arrows represent approximate wind direction and day.

There were other reports and findings flowing in, both right after the sinking, and later. One report that has been cited often and is popular with many is the report from the tug *Reid*, finding a spar protruding from a sunken vessel on the lake bottom. This sighting, along with the reports of the No. 2 off the Ohio coast Tuesday night are primary drivers of the theory that Captain McLeod headed east to Erie or Long Point when he could not safely enter Conneaut harbor.

"The tug Reid, which left here this morning on its way to Conneaut to lay up for the winter, is reported at 3 o'clock this afternoon, to have found a spar of the missing car ferry Bessemer & Marquette No. 2 (reversed in quotation) sticking above the water twelve miles north of Conneaut. (*Erie Times-News*)ᶜᶜᵛ

Erie, Pa, Dec. 17th: "The men and officers of the tug Reid, Capt. Ole Christ commanding, assert that the wreck of the Marquette & Bessemer No. 2, which had 38 persons on board when it steamed from port ten days ago, has been found about 12 miles north of the south shore of Waldemere, a summer resort four miles north of this city. Capt. Christ is said to have notified another tug today while on a trip up the lake, that he discovered the missing boat, a spar of which was alleged to have been sticking out of the water." (*Duluth News-Tribune*)ᶜᶜᵛⁱ

It was not long before this report was refuted by the company in the report below. "The report today that the tug Reid had discovered the wreck of the car ferry Marquette and Bessemer No. 2, which foundered in Lake Erie ten days ago, was discredited by officials of the company here tonight. The report was discredited by an official from the company." (Associated Press)ᶜᶜᵛⁱⁱ I have not found any further information on why this report was found to be not credible. It is implied officials from the company searched the area for wreckage without success.

As I have stated earlier, had the No. 2 sank anywhere off Erie or Conneaut on the Ohio side, I think the strong winds out of the southwest and then directly out of the west would have driven more of the wreckage east, past Long Point, and we would have seen wreckage on the Ohio and Pennsylvania coast. This did not happen. Wreckage did eventually make its appearance on the Ohio coast and further east. First Mate John McLeod's body traveled all the way to Niagara, and one of the No. 2's lifeboats was found broken on the Buffalo break wall, but this did not happen until the following spring, summer and fall. As we saw in Chapter Six, some other bodies were recovered in the Eastern Basin of Lake Erie. I believe strongly that wreckage made its way later via currents and traveling on or in the ice. Some examples of such are included below.

"The signboard of a life raft of the ill-fated Marquette & Bessemer ferryboat No. 2, which foundered last winter, and carried 22 (error in paper) to their death, was picked up yesterday by several boys on the west beach of Point Gratiot." (*Erie Times-News*)[ccviii]

"The captain of an Ashtabula fishing tug today reported that an Erie fisherman had found the wreck of the Marquette & Bessemer No. 2, the car ferry that was lost in the lake last December, with all hands-on board. The Erie man claims that in dragging a net, he caught an ax that bore the name of the car ferry." (*Cleveland Plain Dealer*)[ccix] In this report, the fisherman would not divulge the location. This report is a rumor on top of a rumor. Fishing nets do bring up artifacts from time to time. In the 1960's there was an example of a human skull being brought up in a fishing net. If indeed, an axe from the No. 2 was recovered, it could have traveled some distance on the ice or could have been lost overboard at any point where crewman may have been de-icing the ship.

"More vessel wreckage was picked up on the ice west of here by Fred Green Saturday Afternoon. He was walking on the beach four miles west of Conneaut in an outer jam, he found the top half of a stateroom door, a piece from a cabin roof and a door panel. The outer side of the stateroom door was painted green and the interior white. (This was the color scheme of the No. 2.) On the interior of the door was affixed a porcelain plate marked No. 1. The timber could not be from the Clarion as the steamer had no state rooms." (*Erie Times-News*)[ccx]

It should be noted here that the wreckage found on the Ohio coast took its time getting there. These items were located primarily in the spring, and

I have not seen any reports of wreckage on the Ohio coast immediately after the loss. It was held in the ice or transported via the currents and may not be as instructive as to where the *Marquette & Bessemer* actually sank. Conversely, the wreckage found directly after the sinking was either located in the middle of the lake or on the Canadian shore.

Note that along Long Point there is a clockwise current cycle that would push debris from the west, to the south and east towards Ohio. Between Ashtabula and Cleveland, the current moves in more of a counterclockwise and opposite pattern, pushing debris to the south. In this scenario, I assume that current patterns have stayed consistent over the years. Note here that currents push south away from Long Point toward Erie, Pennsylvania. I was not able to find data for 1910, though I would expect long-term patterns of lake currents to be stable. Note the triangular area with little movement between Ashtabula and Cleveland.

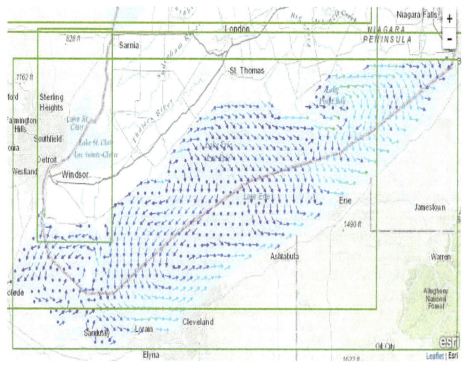

Lake Erie Current Map, National Oceanic and Atmospheric Association.

Then there are two truly amazing reports I had a difficult time believing of the ship being seen under the ice in the spring on the Canadian side of the lake. They may be the same story reported twice, but they differ just enough in the detailas that I have included them both here.

"Around the hotels and stores of the village that parties well known made several trips of exploration across the ice during the winter and that they came upon the great hulk after having proceeded east 8 to 10 miles. The story from Erie, Pa to the effect that the wreck had been sighted off the southern shore was never confirmed, and there are many in Port Stanley who believe that the great coffin of more than a dozen poor sailors will be found not more than ten miles from Port Stanley. The ice is so clear that in many places where it is clear of snow, one can see to a great depth." (*Erie Times-News*)[ccvi] This article gives more detail about the condition of the ice and reports of the ship being off Port Stanley.

Here is the other report of the ship being seen under the ice near the Canadian side. As I have stated, while similar, the details differ sufficiently that I thought they both merited inclusion.

"That the wreck of the car ferry Marquette and Bessemer, which foundered in Lake Erie last December, lies in deep water 14 miles from Port Bruce is the story that has been circulated around Port Stanley during last few days. The report states that a lot of cars, aboard the ferry when she sunk, had been located under the ice off Port Bruce, Ontario, 14 miles from Port Stanley, and that the hulk of the ferry is also visible." (*Buffalo Evening News*) [ccxxii]

When I began researching this book, I was fairly dismissive of these claims. I have not seen much more reporting on this other than the two original stories. The context, the first report implying walking parties, plus the solid nature of the ice imply it was not a ship that made this report. Was someone walking around on the ice 14 miles from shore in the springtime? Perhaps some intrepid, slightly suicidal ice fisherman? This report just didn't seem very believable, despite rewards offered by the Marquette & Bessemer Dock and Navigation Company for finding the vessel and payment for recovered bodies. Regardless, it merits a closer look in the summary because there are parts of it that may fit our physical evidence. It supports one of the more likely narratives of what happened to the No. 2.

Here is another report that definitely caught my attention. It is a tiny article in the *Detroit Free Press* located at the Historical Collection of the

Great Lakes, but one I think is of great importance.

"Cleveland, Ohio, May 16,[th] from information from the search party from Conneaut which has which has been searching for traces of the Marquette & Bessemer No. 2 along the Canadian shore which foundered on Dec. 7th in the vicinity of Long Point. The search party traversed the beach for 26 miles. Part of the side of a freight car, carried from Conneaut (M & B No. 2) on the vessel's last trip, and air tanks from one of her yawl boats were found. Pieces of stateroom doors, window frames and other woodwork were identified as from the lost vessel were discovered 18 miles from Port Rowan." (*Detroit Free Press*)[ccxxiii] The direction from Port Rowan is unclear and it sounds as though vast quantities of wreckage were found along a large swath of the point. A subsequent report in October points to large quantities of wreckage showing up east of Port Rowan, about the tip of Long Point. Though quantities of wreckage were found along a large swath of the point. A subsequent report in October points to large quantities of wreckage showing up east of Port Rowan, about the tip of Long Point. Through May to October of 1910, it appears a vast quantity of wreckage washed up on Long Point. I think this is a significant report. I have included this report even though it duplicate previous reports. Wreckage had been reported along Long Point all that spring. Those sightings may be the same yawl boat air tanks that have appeared in other reports. What caught my attention in this report was "part of a side of a freight car!" In all the material I have read about the loss of the No. 2, this is the ONLY mention I have seen of confirmed wreckage rom a rail car. We have the ghost cars under the ice that, if found at all, apparently could not be found again. I think this information is important for two reasons. First, it, with all the other wreckage signifies the violence of the sinking. Certainly the destruction was sufficient to destroy a rail car.

Many have postulated that the No. 2 sank when its cargo of rail cars broke free, but this is the only report of confirmed rail car wreckage I have found. This evidence suggests the rail cars from the No. 2 did indeed break loose, either as a cause of the sinking, or as a result. This evidence also suggests that the No. 2 did sink stern first. While not absolute proof, for a While not absolute proof, for a rail car to get out of the ship, it would have to jump the track and its wheel lock and then, as had happened previously, the car would head for the stern.

from a rail car. We have the ghost cars under the ice that, if found at all, apparently could not be found again. I think this information is important for two reasons. First, it, with all the other wreckage signifies the violence of the sinking. Certainly the destruction was sufficient to destroy a rail car.

Many have postulated that the No. 2 sank when its cargo of rail cars broke free, but this is the only report of confirmed rail car wreckage I have found. This evidence suggests the rail cars from the No. 2 did indeed break loose, either as a cause of the sinking, or as a result. This evidence also suggests that the No. 2 did sink stern first. There is also the possibility a car punched through the side of the ship, or that the ship capsized, but the presence of this particular piece of wreckage alone, more so than anything else, confirms to me the ship sank stern first. This also somewhat supports the bizarre reports of the rail cars being seen below the ice two months earlier, which initially I doubted.

When I saw this report, I had one more question, and then an epiphany. How does one find a "side" of a rail car? I was especially perplexed by this because the rail cars on the No. 2 were undoubtedly hopper cars, which would be customary for bulk cargo like coal. That is when it occurred to me, could they have been made of wood? Apparently, throughout most of the 19th century, hopper cars were actually made out of wood, and while the last ones were manufactured in 1899, wooden hopper cars remained in service until the 1920's. I had always thought of hopper cars as being the modern steel ones we see today. While it is likely the car ferry had a percentage of these on board, some of the hopper cars must have still been of the wooden construction type. That is a fairly large and meaningful piece of wreckage washing up on the Canadian shore.

It means that at some point, at least one rail car, probably a lot more, found their way out of the wreck. Did this cause the sinking, or was it a byproduct of the ship losing its cargo on the way down? This we cannot know for certain, but I think it makes it much more plausible that the No. 2 may have been dragged down when the cars broke loose. It also may explain, why, at least based on reports, no one with a magnetometer has found a metal rail car lying about. Perhaps there simply weren't that many on the ship, if any.

Port Rowan, Ontario, Oct 8th, 1910: "Two young men here found a piece of wreckage five feet by 16 inches east of the old site of the lifesaving station with the name of the ill-fated Marquette which foundered last fall on one of its life belts (life belt attached to the wreckage?). All sorts of wreckage have come ashore near the same place, including quantities of brass fixtures and such like. From the finding of the captain's body here, it is believed by most that the ill-fated car ferry is someplace on a line directly between Long Point and Erie directly across the lake." (*Erie Times-News*)[ccxxiv] This report is a little confusing as Port Rowan is on the northwest side of Long Point. How could all the wreckage and bodies be on the south shore of Long Point, and then somehow, we have wreckage washing up at Port Rowan? As it turns out, the old Port Rowan lifesaving station was not at Port Rowan physically, but near Port Rowan on Long Point's south facing shore. This makes more sense both because the sheltered waters of Port Rowan itself would be far less likely to need a lifesaving station, and this is also the area where a vast and steady flow of *Marquette & Bessemer No. 2* wreckage and some bodies have found their way onshore. A steady flow of wreckage along this stretch of the Canadian shore between Port Burwell and this area of Long Point supports one of a couple different possibilities for the ship's location. Assuming no change in the lake's current patterns, it should be noted that currents would push wreckage along and down the point, before making a rotation towards the Ohio coast.

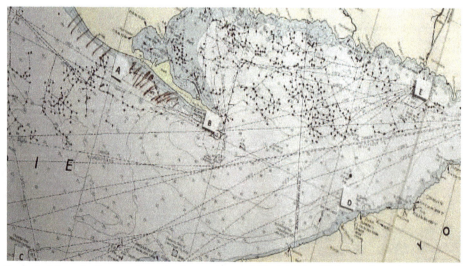

Included here is the wreckage in the spring to fall of 1910. This wreckage is scattered all over the lake. A represents the large spread of wreckage found by the Conneaut party in May. B represents large quantities of wreckage and some bodies, including Captain McLeod's, found in October. C represents wreckage found on the ice west of Conneaut. D represents the horrifically decomposed body found on the resort beach and E indicates bodies and wreckage found in the Eastern basin.

Years Later

Of course, our ghost ship provides more and more clues that add to the mystery as the years have worn on. This includes not one, but two notes in a bottle. One, found in 1914 off Erie, PA, was discredited as a cruel and stupid hoax. It was purported to be from passenger Albert Weis. "The note found in a bottle by two Erie boys Tuesday was not the handwriting of Albert Weis, and the name was misspelled, with the i and the e being transposed. This was the opinion of Henry Hinrichs Jr., of the Keystone Fish Company, when a reporter for the *Times* showed him the bottle and the note Thursday morning. It was thought the whole thing was the work of some practical joker." (*Erie Times-News*)[ccxv]

This was not the only note in a bottle found from the *Marquette & Bessemer No. 2*. Years later, there is another message in a bottle. I am not so sure this one is a hoax.

"A tiny bottle with a message scrawled in pencil on an old magazine cover was found on a beach in Port Stanley in 1928. Barely legible, it said The Bessemer is sinking 15 miles South of Port Stanley." (*Conneaut News-Herald*)[ccxvi] This tiny artifact, other than the ship's ghostly whistle, may be the only word we have really had from the ship since its loss. It boggles the imagination that a tiny bottle might be floating around in the lake for 18 years, only to finally be found. The No. 2 was not equipped with a message case like the S.S. *Milwaukee*, so perhaps this note was hastily composed by one of the bridge officers. It is odd and unfortunate that the note wasn't signed.

The first note is an obvious fraud. This one, I am not so sure about. I think it is odd it is unsigned, but otherwise it is interesting. Perhaps the signature had faded over time. It is one of the many reports that puts the No. 2 somewhere south of Port Stanley. It may truly be the last communication from the No. 2. It does support other evidence that is beginning to accumulate that the No. 2 may indeed have been lost south of Port Stanley.

The clues and red herrings continue to pile up. When I first started researching this story, one of my favorite and most likely accounts was that of the package freighter *Jack*. On initial inspection, it really felt like after all those years, the No. 2 had been found.

In 1932, about 7 PM on July 10,[th] the package freighter *Jack* struck some type of uncharted underwater obstruction on its way from Buffalo to Detroit. This occurred approximately 35 miles southwest of Long Point, breaking of the crank web of the low-pressure cylinder, disabling the ship. The *Jack* ultimately had to be taken under tow several hours later. (*Cleveland Plain Dealer*)[ccxvii]

"Checking a map of the lakes, it was found that the point described by the officers of the Jack corresponds approximately with the place where the car ferry was thought to have gone down." (*Cleveland Plain Dealer*)[ccxviii] What else could the *Jack* have hit? Reporters of the time postulated it could have been the long-lost No. 2. A more precise location would be helpful, but I have been unable to obtain this. The *Jack's* log books would certainly have been helpful, but I have not been able to locate any. We can get an approximation of where this location is with a little deductive reasoning. We can see the normal shipping routes from Buffalo to Detroit on our Lake Erie chart. There are two parallel courses that run relatively close together. We can then take a compass set to the appropriate distance and draw an arc from the Long Point lighthouse (assuming that when they say "off Long Point," that is what they mean) That will give us the best approximation of where the *Jack* hit its obstruction as we will likely ever get. We will also have to presume that the *Jack* was slightly off course when it hit this obstruction, otherwise it or another vessel would have hit this obstruction long before 1932.

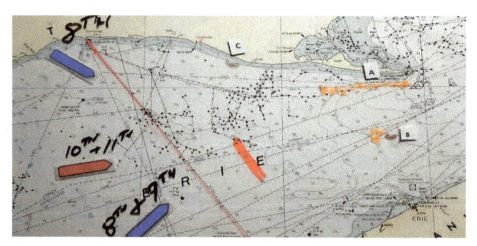

As before, where the *Davock* first encountered wreckage is marked on the chart with the letter B. The letter B marks the location of lifeboat No. 4. The rough location of the No. 2 lifeboat is marked by the letter C. Note that the colored arrows indicate the wind directions on the dates in question. Once again, the thin red line is the course between Conneaut and Port Stanley. The thick red line represents the general area where I think the *Jack* was disabled.

We can approximate the location where the *Jack* hit the obstruction by drawing a 35-mile arc from Long Point and seeing where it intersects the shipping lanes as seen in the thick red line above. We can further narrow some of the possible sites if we assume that the wreck is not in the areas on the map proliferated with gas wells, or it may well have been found already.

Unfortunately, I have not been able to locate more accurate records. As one can see, the main problem with this is that if the many assumptions I have made here are even close to accurate, how did wreckage like the No.2 lifeboat and other items wash up so far north of this location only a day or two after the sinking given the west, northwest and southwesterly winds? Of course, we have a lot of sightings of the No. 2 lifeboat, and the location varies east to west from 8 to 12 miles east of Port Burwell. Given the wide array of assumptions, this may be a plausible location for the No. 2, although it is no longer my favorite. Because with the westerly wind pattern I am not sure how the No. 2 lifeboat could have gotten that far north. Otherwise, this theory would check quite a few boxes.

As I have said, we cannot be positive of the exact location here, nor fully account for local deviations in wind pattern, but I think this is a less likely location, although the Jack did hit something. In the news of the day, it was reported that it would be expected that the obstruction would be marked. It seems this never happened, though one cannot know for sure. This event occurred at the height of the Great Depression, and resources may have been scarce. Like most of the potential locations of the wreck that appear in print, follow up is virtually non-existent.

Ironically, the *Jack*, like the *Marquette & Bessemer No. 2*, was built by the American Ship Building Company in Lorain, Ohio. The *Jack* was originally named the *Lake Fresco* and built in 1919. (Historical Collections of the Great Lakes)[ccxix] The *Jack* also came to a bad end, being torpedoed and sunk by the U-558 between Haiti and Jamacia on May 27, 1942. The Jack was owned by the US Army Transport Service at that time and was carrying a cargo of sugar. 37 were lost, including 8 passengers and the captain. (U-boat net)[ccxx]

An undated, unattributed newspaper clipping (probably from 1957) indicates for the past 8 years residents from Tyrconnell have been using coal that has been washing up on the beaches there. "Residents may be using coal from a ship that sank 48 years ago. The coal is washed up on the shore after every storm with sand and gravel from the lake bottom" Another clipping, year unknown but dated July 18th, possibly from the *Detroit Free Press* indicates coal has been washing up on the beaches two miles west of Port Talbot. It was postulated that this coal was being washed up from deep in the lake and could be from the car ferry. The reality is that the currents will run along the Ontario coast from west to east, carrying objects with it. Storms pushing coal up from deeper waters probably could be from a dozen or more wrecks in the general area. Tyrconnell was a busy port at one time. While not impossible, there is little reason to tie this coal to the car ferry specifically.

"In 1964, Donna Rodebaugh, niece of the captain and first mate, learned that Captain Sam Moore of the fishing tug *Trimac II*, trawling in 145 feet of water in August of 1963, had lost a $600 trawl on some sort of wreck. The chart on his recoding depth finder indicated a rather massive object that jutted up about 45 feet from the bottom. With the graph that Captain Moore turned over to them, and with shoreline reference points provided, they hope to organize an expedition." (Boyer)[ccxxi] It is unclear what became of this lead. There is at least one account of the Rodebaughs launching an expedition to find the No. 2 in deeper water in 1964 but this relates to a different target, a large underwater obstruction off Long Point found by an underwater survey tug. (*The Cleveland Plain Dealer*)[ccxxii] Undoubtedly, there were probably several attempts by the Rodebaugh's to locate the No. 2 as leads trickled in. It appears they were actively searching for the vessel for some time. Unfortunately, they were not successful. In a newspaper interview more than 80 years after the tragedy, Donna Rodebaugh reports "My theory is that there is a fault line at the township or at the state line east of Conneaut, not far out. She (Rodebaugh) Bolsters her theory the ship is in a fault by stating after 80 years, somebody should have found it by now." (*The News-Herald*)[ccxxiii]

"Port Stanley fisherman Larry Jackson believes he has found the wreck and hopes to get salvage rights." (*London Free Press*)[ccxxiv] In 1975, "Jackson contends he has pulled up a rail which fits the description of the car ferry as seen in photographs before the ship went down. The rail was pulled up using mechanical devices. Larry Jackson would not divulge the location and was reportedly seeking salvage rights." (Historical Collection of the Great Lakes)[ccxxv] It is possible that Larry Jackson did indeed pull up part of a railing from a wreck and that it may well have been the No. 2. It is unclear if he was ever able to identify that location accurately again. In Frank Prothero's interview about that time, he states that the rail did very much resemble that of the No. 2 and that there was a fresh break in the metal. He further reports Jackson was known to fish further out in the lake south of Port Stanley. (Elgin County Archives)[ccxxvi] This lead is promising, but like so many instances where our ghost ship has been reported to be found, it has never materialized into anything solid, at least not publicly.

There have been disparate reports of the wreck of the No. 2 being seen from the air 8 miles off Ashtabula in years past. While it is not unusual to be able to spot shipwrecks from the air in the Great Lakes, especially in the spring when the water is clearer, this has never translated to an actual finding of the ship. This has been a sparsely reported story and I do not give it a great deal of credence. Apparently, it has never been confirmed, and I have not been able to determine exactly where this report originated. I do not put a great deal of stock in it both because it has apparently never been verified, but also because I do not believe the wreck will be found off Ashtabula for reasons I have stated previously.

As one can see, there are a vast number of highly scattered physical clues related to the *Marquette & Bessemer No. 2*. Like the mystery of its final hours on the surface, the location of the ship's grave remains elusive. It fades in and out. It may have even been found at points, but then suddenly lost again. The physical evidence is just as confounding in some ways as the reports of the ship or her whistle, but in the next chapter, let us see if we can make some sense of it all.

Chapter 8: Where is She Hiding?

The No. 2 in the ice. Photo Courtesy of the Historical Collection of the Great Lakes, Bowling Green State University.

Between the many, sometimes conflicting, reports of the No. 2, the widely dispersed wreckage, and the fact we have no concrete time for when the ship actually sank, it is not surprising that there are so many divergent theories as to where the No. 2 is resting. The possibilities seem endless, and there are also what seem like endless breadcrumbs of clues, rumors and reports that support wildly different versions of how and where the ship met its end. In this chapter, I will try to summarize these and see if any can be eliminated based on the evidence.

One theory that was proposed around the time of the ship's sinking was that she sank Tuesday afternoon as she tried to execute her turn away from Port Stanley. This was a simple and direct theory that, when I started writing this book, I had entertained. The more I got into the story, the more I saw the potential weaknesses in the boat, it seemed more likely that she would sink quickly and violently. While I am certain some of the reports of the boat's whistle or an actual sighting are at least partially factually incorrect, there are enough of them to convince me the *Marquette & Bessemer No. 2* was still afloat sometime after Tuesday afternoon. Additionally, had the vessel perished Tuesday afternoon on December 7th. I believe that we would have seen wreckage of the ship much sooner than December 10th, and more of it right off and east of Port Stanley, as the prevailing weather was still very strongly from the southwest. Additionally, we know that the No. 2 did successfully launch the No. 4 lifeboat. Should the ship have sunk close off Port Stanley on Tuesday, executing its turn, I think there is a good chance the No. 4 lifeboat would have made it to shore, especially with what was still a prevailing southwest wind behind them. Even as the wind reportedly shifted out of the northwest Wednesday morning, there is an excellent chance they would have made it to Long Point, instead of 64 miles to the southeast, where they were found 15 miles north of Erie. As such, I think we must now regard the possibility that the ship sank off Port Stanley on Tuesday as highly improbable. While based on the physical wreckage, this is a possibility, it just doesn't fit the timeline, and we would have to assume that all the reports of the ship after 5:00 PM Tuesday are inaccurate.

One of the theories I have seen finds the ship turning toward Rondeau when she could not enter Port Stanley at the height of the storm, and that she sank between Port Stanley and Rondeau, or possibly off Rondeau. As I have stated earlier, I think what Mr. Wheeler saw was Captain McLeod executing his turn to port so that he could attempt a return to Conneaut, however, he may have been turning toward Rondeau. This observation may be true and is likely the source of the theory that the ship headed west. It fits the pattern of the wreckage we see in the days after the sinking, but, again, for this to be true, we must discount every report of the ship after Tuesday afternoon, and I still think we would have seen wreckage much earlier and further west.

There was another reason I initially did not believe that the No. 2 foundered between Port Stanley of Rondeau Tuesday night or Wednesday morning. Sometime after Friday's report of the *Davoc* encountering the debris field off Long Point, Charles J. McGill, the superintendent of dock operations, ordered the *Marquette & Bessemer No. 1* to suspend normal operations and look for the No. 2. "The No. 1 was commanded by Captain Murdock Rowan, first cousin to the McLeod brothers and a seaman of vast experience. He took his ship up the north shore to Rondeau, came back to the south shore, which he followed as far as Erie, Pa and then steamed back to the Canadian shore and eastward as far as Long Point. At no time did he sight the No. 2 or any part of her." (Boyer)[ccxxvii] Had the ship sunk on the way to Rondeau or the loop back to the Ohio coast, I had believed it is very likely Captain Rowan would have encountered some kind of wreckage.

It is possible that the No. 2 did indeed head toward Rondeau. I have discovered, however, that despite being reported widely as fact, the *Marquette & Bessemer No. 1* may not have searched for the car ferry.

"It was falsely reported that the No. 1 had been looking for the carferry. The carferry No.1 (really a collier, not a carferry) which has been at Port Rowan since the heavy storm of Tuesday a week ago arrived here Wednesday. The boat took on cargo and again departed. The report was common that the No. 1 was making a search for her missing sister boat. This was not the case and the only search work from the other side was by tugs that were sent out." (*Conneaut News-Herald*)[ccxxviii] It is probable that these search tugs headed toward Rondeau as well as elsewhere. As the No. 2 was seen turning in that direction, it makes sense. This is only an assumption though and not as concrete as before. Still, had the ship sunk on the way to Rondeau on Tuesday or early Wednesday morning, I expect wreckage would have been encountered sooner and found by the search tugs.

Some have theorized that Captain McLeod did indeed head west toward Rondeau, found the harbor no more accessible than Port Stanley, and then turned south to the Ohio shore. The No. 2 then worked her way up the Ohio coast in the lee of the shore to Conneaut where there were reports of her whistle off the harbor, some of which have been refuted, some not. There were also the eyewitness reports of the ship being seen east of the harbor that same night.

One of the appeals of this theory is that it helps account for the large gap in time between the sighting at Port Stanley on Tuesday afternoon until her being heard by the Hulett operator at 1:30 AM Wednesday morning. The nine-and-a-half-hour gap is a large one although it is difficult to imagine it would be possible to cover that distance under those conditions. The *Marquette & Bessemer No. 1*, Captain Rowan's lower profile collier, reported a brutal time getting to Rondeau on Tuesday. "The Marquette and Bessemer No. 1 left Conneaut Harbor at 7:00 AM. It took him 7 hours bucking the waves to cover just the last 7 miles to Rondeau. Winds were gusting to 100 mph and waves were reaching more than 30 feet. Crewmembers said it was the most frightening 7 hours of their lives." (*Lake Erie Beacon*)[ccxxix] The *Conneaut News-Herald* report calls this into question now. It appears the No. 1 did not make it to Rondeau on Tuesday, December 7th after all. Did Captain Rowan attempt it and then turn for the shelter of Port Rowan? Did he not attempt that run at all? This we cannot know with the information available.

What we do know is this account probably accurately reflects conditions at the end of the storm and reflects that the going was undoubtedly slow. I think it is unlikely Captain McLeod would have been able to cover that distance in the time allotted. Additionally, had Captain McLeod turned west, wouldn't he have just kept going toward a larger harbor like Cleveland, Fairport Harbor or Ashtabula?

There is also, I think, an important piece of information to be gleaned here. Captain Rowan and the No. 1 left harbor a couple hours before the No. 2, and it now appears they abandoned their trip to Rondeau at some point during the trip on Dec. 7th and headed for the shelter of Long Point. They were ahead of Captain McLeod and the No. 2 by a couple hours, and the weather was getting progressively worse. If we accept Mr. Wheeler's sighting of the No. 2 off Port Stanley on Tuesday afternoon as factual, and I do, why didn't Captain McLeod make the same decision with a less stable ship under worse conditions? That is when it occurred to me, he didn't think he could. He decided he could not expose his stern to a following sea in those conditions, so he did not turn the boat east at that point. Captain Rowan was not concerned about an open stern, but this was a chance Captain McLeod knew he couldn't take. I think that helps guide us in his decision making going forward. If he decided he couldn't risk it on December 7th, I doubt he was willing to try it later on December 8th or 9th. I now think that Captain McLeod considered a run to the shelter of Long Point untenable under any circumstances. If he can be faulted, it is for taking the ship out in the first place. Once a freighter in front of him was torn from its moorings by the wind, he probably should have just stayed in port. Once he was on the lake, he was committed, and it is becoming clear, his options for maneuver were limited. Regardless of which direction she headed, the ship was undoubtedly taking a battering. Was Captain McLeod taking a loop south from Port Stanley to the Ohio coast? Perhaps Captain McLeod attempted to anchor to ride out part of the storm with his bow facing the wind. I have heard that it is very difficult for vessels with a high freeboard (a large distance between the deck and the water) to successfully anchor in a violent storm, and that is likely that eventually the anchor chains snapped, even if running the ship's engines to keep maximum pressure off the chains. Regardless, this may have been a tactic used by a man trying to buy time. We will never know for sure what transpired during that gap in time. We also cannot be certain that the report of the ship off Conneaut harbor early Wednesday morning is completley credible. Two of these reports, often reported as fact, were later recanted.

As stated earlier, I don't think the ship sank off Port Stanley Tuesday, and that it did not sink off Rondeau. Wreckage would have been seen sooner I believe, and the prevailing southwest winds would have pushed some of it ashore sooner and further west. I think there are enough reports of the ship being heard or seen after Tuesday that she was still afloat on Wednesday. I have stated earlier my reasons for thinking the ship did not sink off the Ohio shore. There are reports of the wind on the Canadian side shifting from the northwest as early as Wednesday morning. (Historical Collection of the Great Lakes)cxxx If the ship sank off the Canadian coast Wednesday morning or later, it's possible the No. 2's flotsam could have been pushed along the coastline before landing on Long Point.

What is important with this part of the story is that it seems very likely the ship made it back to either Conneaut, Port Stanley or both. While I am very interested in telling the story and recounting the history, my stated purpose is to narrow down the location of the vessel to something manageable. For our purposes, there are no witness reports of the ship west of either Port Stanley or Conneaut. This is a remarkable feat for a boat that clearly made itself heard off all the other harbors. The No. 2 may or may not have taken a wide loop west to get back to the Ohio shore, but it doesn't seem she sank on this route both because of the subsequent reports, and because no wreckage was encountered along this route by search tugs, assuming they indeed went that way.

What if, instead of heading to Rondeau, another narrow small harbor channel, Captain McLeod turned to the southwest, heading directly into the wind and on a course to a harbor with better shelter, like Cleveland, Fairport Harbor or Ashtabula? If he simply didn't make it and the boat foundered in the middle of the lake, this would fit the distribution of wreckage we have seen rolling up on the Canadian shore, and a direct westerly wind could have driven the No. 4 lifeboat across the lake to its ultimate location where it was found north of Erie. I think it is a real possibility that we will explore shortly.

This gets us and the No. 2 to early Wednesday morning. While some sightings of the ship by the steamer *Black* and the report of Mr. Brebner hearing the whistle have been recanted, there are still several reports of the boat being seen or heard off Conneaut, Canada, and the Ohio coast about this time. Can they all be wrong? Maybe. For the *Marquette & Bessemer No. 2* to have foundered in the middle of the lake on the way to Cleveland or another Ohio port, all of the subsequent reports of the ship would have to be incorrect. If they are, then the run to Cleveland is an intriguing possibility.

It is hard to expect that every account of the No. 2 off the Ohio coast and subsequent reports of the ship off the Canadian coast are all wrong, though we know some of them have to be. Let us assume for a moment that Captain McLeod was able to make it back to Conneaut. At this point he would have had several different options. He could have run up the coast to Erie, but at this point, I don't think he felt another nighttime approach to harbor in a blizzard was in the cards. Additionally, I now think he was unwilling to expose his stern to boarding seas. He could have turned west into the storm or east, attempting a run towards the shelter of Long Point. The run toward Long Point is the theory proposed by Boyer and many others since the sinking. With winds and waves coming out of the west at this point, I think this would have exposed his stern to a following sea that likely would have swamped the car deck. If he did not take that option on December 7th, aborting his trip like Captain Rowan may have, I couldn't see him selecting that option now. One has to also imagine the condition the boat may have been in at this point. Heavy accumulations of ice may have been weighing down the ship, and it may have been extremely hazardous to send men out on the deck to remove it. Icing of the pilot house windows would have been a significant problem. It is likely that one would have to periodically step out onto the flying bridge for visibility. I think many of the instances of the ship's whistle may have been simply the boat probing for an answering whistle to confirm the presence of a harbor. The ship likely had already taken a lot of water even if the pumps were working at capacity.

That Captain McLeod sought the shelter of Long Point and sank on the way after not being able to access ports on either side of the lake is one of the more common and popular theories of her loss over the years. Additionally, because of the size of the ship, the deeper water in front of Long Point is a more credible hiding spot. Indeed, Captain McLeod may have decided this was his best chance to save his ship. This move would have exposed his stern to boarding seas. Perhaps he hoped the pumps could keep up with it long enough to get to shelter. In this scenario, either water got to her engine room, killing her steam, or her cargo of rail cars broke free as the stern became lowered with the volume of water. Had the boat listed as well, which happened in that harrowing November storm, launching lifeboats may have been difficult. This could also explain the damage to the No. 4 lifeboat. Part of the support of this theory is the location of the No. 4 lifeboat 15 miles

miles due north of Erie, PA. Surely the ship had to be close to where the lifeboat was found.

I do not agree with this theory, however. Had the No. 2 sank that far east, I think the debris field would also have to have been further east because of the prevailing wind out of the west, southwest and northwest. This is also why I discount the ship having gone down off of Conneaut or Erie. The wind would have driven more of the debris east of Long Point, and the westerly winds would have driven more of the debris up the lake's southern shore. Some wreckage did make the Ohio shore, but in the spring of 1910, carried on the ice or by the prevailing currents, not the winds after the storm. This is why I do not think the No. 2 will be found off Erie, along the Ohio Coast or off Long Point. Much more of the significant wreckage would have drifted further east, beyond Long Point at the time of the sinking, not months later as actually happened. Additionally, we cannot then account for how wreckage got west of the proposed sinking site under these conditions. This is also why I do not think the spar reported by the tug *Reid* (later discredited) was the No. 2. More wreckage would have drifted east and wound up on the southern shore. The other thing we have to consider is, if the No. 2 sank off Long Point or off Conneaut or Erie, how did the No. 2 lifeboat get to Port Burwell? One can argue that the wreck probably cannot be far east of the No. 2 lifeboat found off Port Burwell, because of the prevailing winds out of the west and southwest from December 7th to December 10.th The conclusion I have come to is that there is no way a ship can sink that far east, and have wreckage show up that far west. So, the *Marquette & Bessemer No. 2* is not in those locations. I just don't see how it is possible based on the physical wreckage we are looking at. The location of the lifeboats are key indicators to me of where the ship could be.

So where is the wreck? I have three possible scenarios that I will attempt to rank in terms of likelihood. My long shot for the location of the wreck of the No. 2 is the site where the *Jack* collided with an underwater obstruction in 1932, wherever that is exactly. As discussed earlier, there are a great many assumptions that have to be made to arrive at the location. It does check some boxes, however. It would fit the scenario of the ship possibly making a run toward Long Point or the Canadian coast. I think we can also lump "in front of Long Point" in this scenario because we may be talking about a fairly broad area. This is what many thought happened at the time. It would account for most of the wreckage seen right after the sinking, but not all of it.

That pesky No. 2 lifeboat that was found off Port Burwell or Clear Creek either December 10th or 11th, depending on reports, still seems too far north and west for my liking, though with the right local winds it might be possible, but not likely. Prevailing weather right after the sinking likely would not have driven the No. 2 lifeboat that far west and north from the estimated *Jack* collision site. The chart showing my best guess as to where the *Jack* hit an underwater obstruction is already displayed on page 93.

Still, this area is a possibility. We cannot account for all the wind and weather patterns after the sinking. Two things work against this theory. One is that there is a tremendous amount of assumption involved in trying to guess where the *Jack* was disabled. Because of that, it is difficult to judge the idea based exclusively on physical evidence. If the site is where I have estimated, some of wreckage may be too far north and west. If current patterns have not changed greatly in Lake Erie over the years, then currents running over this area would move along Long Point in a clockwise pattern, turning south toward Ohio. Because of this pattern, if we use the *Jack* collision site as a prospective location of the wreck, I think more of the of the subsequent wreckage would have been pushed south toward the Ohio coast. It does fit the large quantities of wreckage that washed up at the tip of Long Point in October of 1910, but not so much the array of wreckage found all along Long Point in the spring of 1910. Additionally, I think we would see the currents drive more wreckage to the Ohio shore in 1910 from this site. There really wasn't a large amount of it, unlike the Canadian shore. While this theory does have its appeal, and I think if we expand it to a sinking in front of Long Point in general, I now think it would put the wreck too far to the south. It is no longer one of my favorite theories. That No. 2 lifeboat still bothers me. One other consideration is depth — about 68 to 70 feet in this section of the lake. Assuming a draft of 20 feet on the *Jack*, the wreck of the No.2 would have to be upright and likely jutting from the bottom for the *Jack* to hit it. Perhaps in the end, it was tree trunk or some other object floating under the surface that disabled the *Jack*.

Part of the appeal of the *Jack* collision site is it does allow us to account for some of the Ohio reports of the ship, but in this scenario, it seems unlikely the No. 2 would have been off Port Stanley or Port Bruce at 5:00 AM Wednesday or Thursday as the ship would have been too far south in this scenario.

The following theory I like more, and that is that the No. 2 made a run to Cleveland or another Ohio harbor to the southwest. On Tuesday afternoon after the No. 2 turned to port, what if Captain McLeod was heading not to Rondeau, but opted instead to turn the ship into the wind to make a run for a major port like Cleveland, Fairport Harbor or Ashtabula, and he simply didn't make it, sinking somewhere in the middle of the lake? This explanation checks a few boxes. If the ship sank near the international border in the middle of the lake on a southwest heading, that puts it in an area of low ship traffic and an area harder for recreational divers to reach. This theory may well account for the evasiveness of our ghost ship.

As one can see on the chart, this is also an area of low gas well activity. It is assumed that the wreck is not in areas densely packed with gas wells because it would have been found, and there is plenty of area free of gas wells in this section of the lake. This is also an area that that would not likely have been searched by the army of fishing tugs out looking for the No. 2. Another important plus for this scenario is that the physical evidence mostly fits. The location of the wreckage of lifeboat No. 4, north of Erie, the debris field off Long Point and the wreckage off Port Burwell, all could have originated from this wreck site, even if the No. 4 lifeboat had been launched early. Should the No. 4 lifeboat have been launched in this area, it would have drifted a considerable distance, approximately 73 miles to where it was found. That seems like a great distance, but assuming an estimated sinking time between midnight and 6:00 AM Wednesday morning and the lifeboat being found early Sunday, that timing gives the lifeboat over 48 hours to cover that distance. With gale force westerly winds, that still is only a pace of 1.5 miles per hour. That seems plausible. This course would also give Captain McLeod a course heading into the wind on December 7th and the early morning of December 8th. There is one small passage in Boyer's book that is interesting. "A couple of years after she 'went missing,' as the second *Marquette & Bessemer No. 2* was beating her way to Rondeau, she touched a large, uncharted underwater obstruction. What could it be but the first car ferry?" (Boyer)[ccxxxi] What this report doesn't say is where the second car ferry is coming from. It is also unclear how he knew this information. Given his experience as a reporter, it may be an oral history or a more obscure source. If we assume the ship was doing the ship's normal business, then it was taking coal from Conneaut to Canada, in this case Rondeau. If it was following this course, it could have "touched" the wreck of the original No. 2 in this area in the middle of the lake.

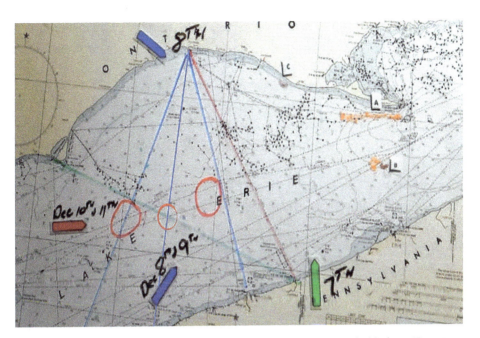

Possible course directions, reported wind directions and debris fields from Dec. 7 through December 11.

As before, the arrows represent wind direction. The green line represents the course from Conneaut to Rondeau where the replacement ferry may have traveled, but this is not completely certain. The blue lines represent runs from Port Stanley to Cleveland, Fairport Harbor or Ashtabula. Here we assume Captain McLeod did not turn toward Rondeau when he turned to port outside Port Stanley, but instead turned toward Cleveland. The red circle on the left represents where the replacement *Marquette & Bessemer No. 2* may have "touched" an underwater obstruction on the way to Rondeau, making this area our probable sinking location in this scenario. The middle red circle on the chart indicates where this may have occurred had the original No.2 sank on the way to Fairport Harbor. The circle on the right marks a possible sinking site if the No. 2 was headed to Ashtabula instead. This area was chosen more arbitrarily. I have selected it because it is another open section in the middle of the lake. On this route, we do see a potential location where a boat traveling from Conneaut to Rondeau could touch an underwater object, however, as I have stated previously, this is too far south for my taste. We would have gotten some earlier wreckage on the Ohio Coast. had the No. 2 sank that far south, and likely earlier. Additionally, I think if it were that close to shore, surely someone would have found the big ship by now.

This scenario checks all of the boxes in terms of wind direction after the sinking, which would drive wreckage east. All of wreckage found after the sinking could be accounted for in this scenario.

There are a couple drawbacks with this location, however. For it to work, we must discount every eyewitness report after Tuesday afternoon. The other factor, in my mind, is that this does seem like a great travel distance for some of the heavier wreckage that eventually appeared on the Long Point beaches in the spring, such as a section of rail car and brass fittings. There is one further problem. If we go back to our map of the lake currents and examine this location on the current map, it seems that we should have gotten at least some wreckage making the Ohio shore further west, at least to Ashtabula, and maybe further toward Fairport Harbor and Cleveland. This didn't happen. It seems possible that with this location, we could see the wreckage we got in the eastern part of the lake, but I would also expect at least some further west from this sinking location. As the current runs along the Ohio coast once it gets close, perhaps the wreckage was simply carried further east before washing ashore. This we cannot know.

Regardless, the ship running southwest to an Ohio port is my strong runner up for where the wreck is. Had the No. 2 sank in this area sometime early Wednesday morning, overwhelmed by the waves, or a victim of its own cargo, it might be able to hide in this area indefinitely, sleeping away the decades.

This scenario gets us to what I think is the most probable location for the wreck. It has been actually the one that has been shouting at us through the decades. After not being able to get into Port Stanley, I think Captain McLeod did indeed turn his ship back toward Ohio. There are enough reports of the *Marquette & Bessemer No. 2* off the Ohio coast, that they can't all be fabrications, can they? Conventional wisdom of the time was that the ship then ran for shelter of Long Point, sinking somewhere between the Ohio shore and there, or that the ship tried to make a run toward Erie, and sank on the way there. As I have said previously, I do not believe the wreck could be this far east based on the physical wreckage, though if far enough off Long Point and west, our first two scenarios are a possibility.

I do believe that the ship headed north after making the Ohio coast, but with a twist. I do not think Captain Mcleod was trying to make it around Long Point. I suspect the prospect of seas boarding his open stern would have been too daunting a chance to take. I think he was heading northwest of the point, possibly on a northwest course from the Girard, Ohio encounter.

Again, the veracity of any of these sightings and their complete accuracy must be taken into account, but we have multiple reports here, which increases our odds the ship was off the Ohio shore. There are the two accounts of a ship heading towards shore in this area.

Here we must use a little imagination. It is the middle of the night in a blinding snowstorm in 1909. Undoubtedly cities were not illuminated as they are today, and harbors and channels not as well marked. The repeated ship's whistle may have been a call to confirm any light that the captain did see that night as a harbor. Navigation must have been extremely difficult. Let us assume for a minute that on Tuesday afternoon, the ship could not make the approach at Port Stanley in daylight because the channel is fairly narrow, and the weather was far too rough. Even if he managed to pile the ship up on a breakwater, there had to be little hope his crew could be rescued under those circumstances. Then, let us assume some of the reports of the ship being off Conneaut early Wednesday morning are correct. Captain McLeod deemed the harbor was too dangerous to enter. There may or may not have also been a ship anchored outside the harbor, more likely the *Mecham* or even some other unidentified vessel. Perhaps he was not actually able to locate the channel that cleanly and was turned away from the shore east of Conneaut. He may have even attempted to anchor off Conneaut unsuccessfully, which fits with William Rice's account of events.

Instead of turning northeast toward Long Point, I think Captain McLeod took the boat back out into the open lake (a reasonable decision given that he may have just nearly run aground at least once), steering a northwest course off the Ohio shore back toward Port Stanley. This may have bought him time; also, it would protect the stern somewhat from weather out of the west. As he worked across the lake, he may have even encountered wind that was starting to build out of the northwest. We have one report of a northwest wind at Port Stanley as early as Wednesday morning. The reality is we are looking at weather reports that are over 100 years old. We can use these to get a good idea of what is happening, but there may be a variance or two locally for points during the storm. Further, it seems the maps from the Agriculture Department were focused primarily on American weather. It does appear we had a northwest wind arising out of Port Stanley Wednesday morning. The end game of this delaying action would be a daytime run at Port Stanley under weather conditions that would hopefully be better in a few hours. Typically, storms on the Great Lakes did not last several days like this one did. If nothing else, Captain McLeod may have been thinking he had a better chance of saving his crew closer to shore in the daylight.

I do not think running out of coal would have been a concern for the No. 2. It would not have been easy, but if it became an issue, I am confident the officers and crew would have figured out a way to cannibalize coal from one of the rail cars on the cargo deck. You will recall Ernest McLaren's harrowing account of survival on page 52, where his ship nearly ran out of coal after 60 hours in the storm. The No. 2 had not been out 48 hours yet, so coal should not have been a problem. It is possible her boilers simply flooded out from the violent seas crashing onto the car deck from whatever angle.

It is along this course I believe the No. 2 sank. She may have gotten trapped in pack ice which may have been forming out on the lake, or simply battered into submission by an accumulation of ice on the boat and taking on more water than the pumps could handle. I do not think this was how the end came though.

I think the ship went down quickly and violently. After the report of the finding of a part of a freight car on the beach at Long Point, I believe the key holding the rail cars in place finally failed, and a string of rail cars plunged off the stern of the ship, flooding her and sinking her quickly. How else did part of a freight car get out of the ship? It could, of course, have broken free on the way down, but based on what we know, I think the rail cars were what finally finished her off. I also think she went down sometime between midnight and 6 AM Wednesday morning, about the same time the off-duty crew was taking to the No. 4 lifeboat.

It is possible the crew had just enough time during the sinking to launch the No. 4 lifeboat, or it is possible they launched the boat early without orders. We will never know for sure. I do not believe Captain McLeod had left the bridge of the vessel or that he was in an altercation with his crew. I could believe crew members gripped with fear could be willing to take a chance on a lifeboat. This is exactly what happened with both the *Clarion* and the *Richardson*, paying tribute to what a terrifying storm this was. As stated earlier, the lifeboat was launched in haste regardless, at half capacity, with no officers, and without proper clothing or supplies. It also appears to have been the only boat that was manned. Along this course, she may have gotten close enough again to Port Stanley or Bruce to be heard. She may have been trying to find her way in the blinding snowstorm.

We may never know for sure what all transpired during those last hours on the lake. I believe that the Marquette & Bessemer No.2 sank sometime between midnight and 6 A.M. either early Wednesday morning or Thursday morning. It is during this period when the men found in lifeboat No.4 were reported to be off duty. John McLeod's watch was reported to be stoppd at 12:25 when his body was recovered. Might this indicate a sinking shortly after midnight? We cannot be sure based on the information we have. The timeline of reports of the ship or it's whistle make a true timeline difficult. The ship may hve gone down as late as sometime Thursday, perhaps after being disabled or trapped in pack ice. An excellent case can be made for my second scenario, that the ship sank early Wednesday morning on a run to a southwest Ohio port. I think, however, the wreck will be found south of Port Stanley. I think she was coming up from the southeast and will be found somewhere in the arc 10 to 15 miles or so southeast of the harbor. There are several reasons why I believe this is true.

The first and foremost is the location of the physical wreckage located immediately after the sinking. Surely the No. 4 lifeboat and the wreckage located by the *Davock* fit this location nicely. It is easy to see the prevailing winds out of the west and northwest driving the wreckage to its ultimate destination. The location of the No. 2 lifeboat is a little trickier. It really doesn't fit as tightly into the weather patterns we know, but it still seems very plausible it traveled east from the wreck site and wound up ultimately 8 miles or more east of Port Burwell. This especially fits if the theories of the lifeboat breaking free of the wreck after its sinking are accurate. If that did indeed happen, and I believe it did, the No. 2 lifeboat could have popped up to the surface a day later with other wreckage. A westerly wind could have driven it directly east from the wreck site to the Port Burwell area. It would account for the shorter distance traveled from the wreck site and its ultimate location.

Secondly, it does not require us to dismiss latter reports of the ship's whistle or its sightings. While some of them can't possibly be accurate based on the timelines we are looking at, we are able to accept that some of them after Tuesday afternoon are indeed factual.

Another reason we can narrow this down as a probable location is that prevailing currents would drive large amounts of wreckage and the bodies of Captain McLeod and Wheelsman Wilson, that may have broken free from the ship later, or spent the winter entombed in the ice, up on the beach between Port Burwell and the expanse of Long Point. This is exactly what happened. This included large pieces of wreckage such as our side of a railcar, and more dense wreckage like the brass fittings that were reported. Further, if we assume the lake currents in 1909 are little changed from today, the currents will travel in a clockwise motion along Long Point before turning south and bouncing off the Ohio coast before traveling east. This pattern would drive more wreckage up on Long Point from this location, but would also account for wreckage and human remains, including John McLeod's body, that missed Long Point and were subsequently carried further south and east to Ohio and along the lake as far as Buffalo, where the broken remains of one of the lifeboats was found, or the water intake at Niagara, where First Mate McLeod was ultimately recovered.

In addition, we have some reports that actually fit this scenario. The outrageous reports that men on the ice in the spring of 1910 actually saw the wreck and its cargo of railcars through the ice: what if those reports are true? Those reports put the wreck about 14 or 15 miles south of Port Stanley and 8 to 10 miles from Port Burwell. This is just within the distance where the ship's whistle could have been heard, as numerous reports have indicated. I have been in parts of Canada where the water clarity is tremendous, and visibility is such that one can see the bottom in fairly deep water. Undoubtedly, water visibility in 1910 was likely far greater than today, and water visibility is best in Lake Erie in the early spring. Further, the depths in this area are fairly uniform in that they are only 16 to 20 meters (54 to 67 feet). It is not outrageous to think the ship could be seen at that depth in the right conditions.

Insurance underwriter Perry Jones at this time offered a $500.00 reward for locating the wreck, so it is conceivable there were parties out on the ice looking for her that winter. (*Erie Times-News*)[ccxxxii] Other rewards had been offered as well. It is also conceivable they were not able to find the exact site again, chose not to disclose it, or simply were not believed. That was certainly my initial impression upon reading those accounts. I grant you that it takes a leap of faith and the suspension of a certain amount of disbelief, but I think that the account may be true. It fits nicely with the other evidence.

Then there is the message in the bottle that washed up on a Port Stanley beach in 1928. This was reported to be badly faded and barely legible, but reported the No. 2 going down 15 miles south of Port Stanley. Is this the last word from our ghost ship? I think perhaps it is. I would prefer the note were signed, although the signature may have simply faded after that many years in the lake. Here we have another piece of information that puts the wreck about 15 miles south of Port Stanley, assuming the note is legitimate, and the *Marquette & Bessemer No. 2* had a decent fix on her own position.

111

Captain McLeod was widely regarded as one of the best navigators on the Great Lakes, so once again, I am going to take a great leap of faith here and assume the note is legitimate. It fits nicely with the other information we have.

Then there is fisherman Larry Jackson, pulling up a portion of railing by mechanical means in 1975. He was convinced enough that he had found the No. 2 somewhere off Port Stanley that he filed for the salvage rights. Did he really find a portion of railing of the No. 2? With the information available, we have no way to answer that question for sure, but I think perhaps he did. If true, here is another clue that puts our ghost ship somewhere off the Canadian shore in the vicinity of Port Stanley. I think our most likely scenario is that Captain McLeod was running back toward Port Stanley and ran out of time. This is the location that checks all the boxes and fits our weather patterns, wreckage, currents, and many of the eyewitness accounts. Additionally, it fits many of the subsequent reports we have seen, some more fantastic that others. I think the wreck will be found somewhere in the ten-to-fifteen-mile arc south of Port Stanley. This location also fits nicely with the heavy wreckage that has washed up later, well after the wreck was lost. It seems it may even have been found briefly in this area, only to escape final detection, like a ghost on the bottom.

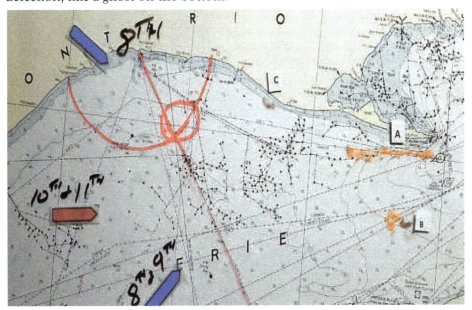

Chart with the circle marking the author's estimate of the likely resting place of the *Marquette & Bessemer No. 2*.

I think the wreck will be found somewhere in the ten-to-fifteen-mile arc south of Port Stanley. This location also fits nicely with the heavy wreckage that has washed up later, well after the wreck was lost. It fits reasonably well with the eyewitness reports we have. This location also has several unusual reports that point there, including the finding of the wreck and rail cars under the ice, and the haunting message in the bottle, which truly may be a communication from the grave.

Possibly she is hiding elsewhere. Perhaps one of the other two scenarios I have outlined are true. Perhaps even one of the scenarios I have outright rejected is true. Such is the nature of performing an autopsy on a shipwreck that occurred under mysterious circumstances with confounding clues over 110 years ago. I know I found it a more complicated problem than I expected, and I changed my thinking several times during the course of this investigation. Regardless, I think that the boat hiding south of Port Stanley is the best bet. Exactly what time she sank is a harder question to answer. I think it was after 5:00 AM Wednesday or early Thursday Morning, perhaps a few hours after she was heard of the Canadian coast. I do not think she sank on Tuesday afternoon for the reasons we have already discussed.

Epilogue/Conclusion

The Marquette & Bessemer No .2 firing up.
Unpublished photo as far as I know. Photo Courtesy of the Historical Collection of
the Great Lakes, Bowling Green State University.

While a record setting success in terms of cargo moved, the 1909 shipping season also exacted a brutal, and in retrospect, a possibly avoidable cost in ships, officers and crew, both experienced and some who probably never should have been put in the positions they were in. Life on the lakes would continue to be a dangerous undertaking for many years, but some positive changes were realized after this brutal year. Some companies were more proactive than others. "That something will be done to stop sailing on the lakes in December is certain, whether the underwriters take any action or not. So long as I am connected with the Pittsburgh Steamship Company, said President Coulby yesterday, navigation for this company will end November 30th. No boats of our fleet will be loaded, nor will we charter any outside tonnage to load after that date." (*The Duluth Evening Herald*)[ccxxxiii]

The advent of wireless, better equipment and training, and critically for railroad car ferries, the addition of stern gates, would improve safety as the years wore on. But the pressure to sail, in good economic times and especially bad, would continue to be great Many more lives would be lost over the years as Great Lakes shipping would play a critical role building the United States into an industrial superpower that just a few decades later

.

would become the arsenal of democracy. The wreck of the Marquette &
Bessemer No. 2 remains elusive, though I feel it will be found soon. She is
hidden well wherever she is. So many rumors and stories about the ship's
finding have been reported over the decades, that perhaps she has already
been located, perhaps by some diver who has taken the location to the
grave. Perhaps, at least briefly, she was found by the intrepid explorers on
the ice inthe spring of 1910 or a myriad of others. This we may never know.
If someone does actually know where the ship is and has been keeping it
close to the vest, I urge them to share their information. It is not a treasure
ship. Albert Weis's briefcase, if it ever existed in the first place, is long gone.
If someone has clues that they can share with others, a collaborative effort
will increase the chances she is discovered. What little I know about wreck
hunters is that they can be a secretive bunch, but it is time to know what
truly happened to this ship. Part of me will be saddened at the loss of a great
mystery, but it is time.

Some feel that she may be silted in or hiding in a fissure. This is not
without precedent. The C.B. Lockwood was a 300-foot wooden steamer
that sank off Grand River, Ohio in October 1902. The wreck was marked
with a buoy and extensively surveyed after it sank, but for decades was lost
to history. (*News Editor*)[ccxxxiv] After years of searching, only an occasional
lifeboat davit, cabin roof, or pipe was found. On August 7th, 2010, the
C.B. Lockwood was found using a sub bottom profiler. The lost ship was
found to be buried in silt, with the top of the vessel being 15 feet under the
bottom silt, in its original location. It never actually left. It is theorized that
earthquake activity, which is common in this area, coupled with the soft lake
bottom facilitated the ship sinking into the muck. (*Master Mario*)[ccxxxv] Some
think this is also the fate of the *Marquette & Bessemer No. 2,* and that is why
she has never been found. While at this point, anything is possible, a ship
being completely engulfed by bottom silt is a pretty rare event that appears
to require a set of very specific conditions. As noted previously in her 1986
interview, this is what Donna Rodebaugh had theorized this was a possibility,
and that was before we had a working example in the C.B. Lockwood. As it is
not a common occurrence it should be considered unlikely. I am hopeful this
is not what happened to the *Marquette & Bessemer No. 2.*

It is theorized earthquake activity is a requisite for this type of event. As I have stated, I do not think the No. 2 is off the Ohio coast, where earthquake activity appears to be most prevalent. While I do not think the wreck is entombed in bottom silt and muck, it probably is somewhat silted in and presents a lower profile than it did in life. Two examples of car ferry wrecks we have today are the S.S. Milwaukee and the Pere Marquette No. 18, which are both sitting upright. Perhaps we will find the No. 2 in such a state as well. We do have reason to believe the ship's sinking was violent, and that there were large quantities of debris on the lake and shorelines. I expect when the wreck is found, much of the woodwork including her pilot house and upper cabins will be gone. I expect at least some of the rail cars, if not all, will be outside the hold of the ship, either from causing the sinking or as a result of it.

Undoubtedly, the wreck will be a ghostly site, standing watch over some of the crew and passengers who are most likely still entombed there. The wreck stands as a time capsule to look into another time, and a monument to all who served on the Great Lakes, including her crew, whether she is ever found or not.

Bibliography

Books

Babbish, Byron, (2017), Erie, Ontario, and All the Others, *Carferries of the Great Lakes*, Create Space, an Amazon Company, pg. 1, pp.12, 32, p.5.

Boyer, Dwight, (1968), *Ghost Ships of the Great Lakes*, NY, NY, Dodd-Mead, pp. 154, 152,1 60, 94, 91,168,147,146.149,148,156,162,155, 157,164.167,165.170.

Hilton, George W, (1962), *The Great Lakes Carferries*, Howell-North Books, Berkeley, CA, pp. 210, 211, 7

Periodicals

The Buffalo Evening News, Buffalo, NY.
May 2,[nd] 1910.
April 7,[th] 1910.
March 12,[th] 1910, Lost Car Ferry May be Off Port Bruce.

The Butler Citizen, Butler, PA.
December 14,[th] 1909, p. 8.

The Cleveland Plain Dealer, Cleveland, OH.
December 13,[th] Nine Bodies Brought in From the Carferry Wreck, 1909, p. 1.
December 11,[th] 1909, Paine Towed into Port.
December 14,[th] 1909, Ill Fated Car Ferry Close to Harbor Vessel Whose Crew of 32 Men Perished.
December 13,[th] 1909, Bodies of Nine Brought in From the Wreck of the Carferry Lost in Great Strom, p. 2.
December 8,[th] 1909, Delayed by Low Water.
December 8,[th] 1909, Marine News.
May 15,[th] 1910, The Ugly Secret Tucked Away in a Little Inland Sea, p. 60.

May 17,[th] 1928, Clew to The Fate of the Bessemer, OH, p. 1.
November 26,[th] 1989, Lake Erie's Wrath Felt 80 Years Ago.
December 16,[th] 1909, No. 1 did not search for the No. 2. p. 1

The Detroit Free Press, Detroit, MI.

December 19,[th] 1909, 30 Boats Total Loss This Year.
December 18,[th] 1909, Swimmer Frozen in a Cake of Ice.
May 17,[th] 1910, May Search for the Bessemer.

The Duluth Evening Herald, Duluth, MN.

December 11,[th] 1909, Fifty-Nine Lives Lost in the Storm on Lake
Erie, p. 1.
February 12,[th] 1910, Over 65,000 Trains Would be Needed to
Transport Freight Handled in Duluth Superior Harbor in
1909.
January 13,[th] 1910, Wissahickon is Released, Duluth Minnesota.
December 11,[th] 1909, Fifty-Nine Lives Lost in the Storm on Lake
Erie.
December 13,[th] 1909. Would Cut the Season.
January 19,[th] 1910. Talks of Raising Premiums.
December 18,[th] 1909, Car Ferry Wreck Found Near Erie, pg. 10.
December 15,[th] 1909, The Season on The Lakes.

The Duluth Labor World, Duluth, MN

February 4,[th] 1910. Incompetents Caused Loss of Richardson
February 5,[th] 1910.

The Erie Times-News, Erie, PA.

December 13,[th] 1909.
December 21,[st] 1909. Car Ferries to be Equipped with Wireless,
p. 1
December 15,[th] 1909.
December 15,[th] 1909, p. 12.
December 16,[th] 1909, O'Hagan Not on Ferry, p. 5.
December 11,[th] 1909, Erie Man on the Carferry, p. 16.
December 13,[th] 1909, pg. 2.
December 16,[th] 1909, Will Take Another Chance, p. 3.

December 15,th Did the Car Ferry Turn Back to Conneaut Harbor, p. 12.

December 16,th 1909. Saw Car Ferry Near Shore, p. 3.

December 13,th 1909, Nine Storm Victims Found Floating in Icy Yawl Boat, p. 1.

April 30,th 1910, Find Another Victim, p. 9.

July 26,th 1910, Floater May be Victim of the Ferry Wreck. p. 1.

October 7,th 1910, Body of Captain M'Leod of Carferry Found. p. 6.

December 13,th 1909, Curled Up in the Bottom of the Boat, p. 1.

October 3,rd 1910, Body Found Not That of Albert Weis, p. 6.

December 10,th 1909, Car Ferry Conneaut Probably Gone Down.

December 17,th 1909, Missing Car Ferry Located, p. 6.

April 1,st 1910, Carferry Wreckage is Found by Boys, p. 4.

March 15,th 1910, Divers May Search for the Lost Carferry, p. 5.

March 11,th 1910, Wreck of the Ill-Fated Car Ferry Found, p. 12.

October 8,th 1910, Believe Carferry sunk of this city, p. 2.

April 23,rd 1914, Practical Joker Wrote Message, p. 3.

March 15,th 1910, Divers May Search for the Lost Ferry, p 5.

The Evening Free Press, London, ON.

December 13,th 1909. Ex-Wheelsman Tells How Cars Broke Loose Once.

December 10,th 1909. John King, A Londoner on Missing Bessemer Joined Boat Recently.

December 10,th1909 Capt. M'Leod has great reputation

December 13,th 1909, McLeod Controlled His Boat as A Women Manages a Go-Cart. p. 1.

December 13,th 1909, Three Members of the Crew are Safe.

December 13,th 1909, Lake Pilot Says Bessemer Sunk if She Attempted to Turn Around. p. 1.

December 13,th 1909, PM Carferry No19 Will Take Bessemer's Place on Lake Run.

December 13,th 1909, Ferry Went Down But A Few Miles Out, p.1.

December 16,th Minister of Marine Orders Probe of Bessemer Wreck.

December 17,th 1909, In Waking Vision Saw Bessemer Sink.

December 13,th 1909, Body of Roy Hinds Among Those Brought into Port on Monday.

December 11,th Farmers Find Bessemer Boat and Wreckage.

December 15,[th] Did the Car Ferry Turn Back to Conneaut Harbor, p. 12.
December 16,[th] 1909. Saw Car Ferry Near Shore, p. 3.
December 13,[th] 1909, Nine Storm Victims Found Floating in Icy
Yawl Boat, p. 1.
April 30,[th] 1910, Find Another Victim, p. 9.
July 26,[th] 1910, Floater May be Victim of the Ferry Wreck. p. 1.
October 7,[th] 1910, Body of Captain M'Leod of Carferry Found. p. 6.
December 13,[th] 1909, Curled Up in the Bottom of the Boat, p. 1.
October 3,[rd] 1910, Body Found Not That of Albert Weis, p. 6.
December 10,[th] 1909, Car Ferry Conneaut Probably Gone Down.
December 17,[th] 1909, Missing Car Ferry Located, p. 6.
April 1,[st] 1910, Carferry Wreckage is Found by Boys, p. 4.
March 15,[th] 1910, Divers May Search for the Lost Carferry, p. 5.
March 11,[th] 1910, Wreck of the Ill-Fated Car Ferry Found, p. 12.
October 8,[th] 1910, Believe Carferry sunk of this city, p. 2.
April 23,[rd] 1914, Practical Joker Wrote Message, p. 3.
March 15,[th] 1910, Divers May Search for the Lost Ferry, p. 5.

The Evening Free Press, London, ON.
December 13,[th] 1909. Ex-Wheelsman Tells How Cars Broke Loose
Once.
December 10,[th] 1909. John King, A Londoner on Missing
Bessemer Joined Boat Recently.
December 10,[th]1909 Capt. M'Leod has great reputation
December 13,[th] 1909, McLeod Controlled His Boat as A Women
Manages a Go-Cart. pg. 1.
December 13,[th] 1909, Three Members of the Crew are Safe.
December 13,[th] 1909, Lake Pilot Says Bessemer Sunk if She
Attempted to Turn Around. p. 1.
December 13,[th] 1909, PM Carferry No19 Will Take
Bessemer's Place on Lake Run.
December 13,[th] 1909, Ferry Went Down But A Few Miles Out,
p.1.
December 16,[th] Minister of Marine Orders Probe of Bessemer
Wreck.
December 17,[th] 1909, In Waking Vision Saw Bessemer Sink.
December 13,[th] 1909, Body of Roy Hinds Among Those
Brought into Port on Monday.
December 11,[th] Farmers Find Bessemer Boat and Wreckage.

April 7,[th] 1910, Body of Bessemer Captain is Found, p. 1.

The Flint Journal, Flint, MN.
December 17,[th] 1909.
December 18,[th] 1909, Wirtz Taking Last Trip, p. 8.

Grand Rapids Press, Grand Rapids, MI.
December 13,[th] 1909, Fifty Float in Lake, Grand Rapids Press. p 1.
December 13,[th] Fifty Float in Lake, Grand Rapids Press, Grand Rapids, MI, p. 5.

The Historical Collection of the Great Lakes, Bowling Green State University, Bowling Green, Ohio.
Unknown, undated newspaper article. Marquette & Bessemer No. 2 folder No. 2.
December 13,[th] 1909, or there abouts. Declares Bessemer "Ghastly Mantrap.", This article is probably from *The Evening Free Press* in London, Ontario, but this cannot be definitely confirmed. Historical Collection of the Great Lakes, Marquette & Bessemer No. 2 folder No. 2
December 17,[th] 1909, Associated Press Dispatch, No Wreckage of the Bessemer II Found. Newspaper unknown. Marquette & Bessemer No.2 folder, retrieved, August 10th, 2022.

The Lake Erie Beacon
Hibbert, Andrew, November 13,[th] 2009, Part 1: Where is the No. 2?
November 13,[th] Lake Erie Beacon, p. 3.
Hibbert, Andrew, November 13,[th] 2009, Part 1: Where is the No. 2? pp. 3-5.
Hibbert, Andrew, November 13,[th] 2009, Part 1: Where is the No. 2? pp. 3-6.

The London Free Press, London, ON.
May 1,[st] 1975, Wreck Believed Found.

News Editor
The Mystery of the CB Lockwood, https://ontariomarineheritage committee.ca/the-mystery-of-the-c-b-lockwood/, March 2017.

The Northern Mariner
Daley, Matthew Lawrence (Spring, 2018). An Unequal Clash: The Lake Seamen's Union, The Lake Carrier's Association, and the Great Lakes Strike of 1909. The Northern Mariner, XVIII, No. 2, pp. 125, 126,132, 136-137.

The St. Thomas Daily Times, St. Thomas, ON.
December 13,[th] 1909. He did not Feel Secure.
December 14,[th] 1909, Couldn't Ship Enough Water.
December 13,[th] 1909, One of Bessemer's Victims New Sarum Lad.
December 13,[th] 1909, December 13th, 1909, p. 1
December 11,[th]1909, Painful Accident was Lucky for Michael, p. 1
December 14,[th] 1909, Seas Ran Too High, p. 1.
December 13,[th] 1909, Heard Distress Whistles.
December 13,[th] 1909, Nine Frozen Bodies Found, One Was Port Stanley Boy, p. 1.
December 13,[th] About Finding Three Bodies, Yawl Boat Not Seen by Port Burrell Boat Winner.

The St. Thomas Journal, St. Thomas, ON.
December 11,[th] 1909.

The Simcoe Reformer, Simcoe, ON.
December 16,[th] 1909, Many Lives Lost on Lake Erie, Ontario, p. 1.

The Star Beacon, Ashtabula, ON.
Ellsworth, Catherine, Marquette & Bessemer Story Set Straight, November 3,[rd] 1986, p. 2.

The Toledo Blade, Toledo, OH
Wooden Vessels Rapidly Vanishing on the Great Lakes, March 12,[th] 1910.
March 12,[th] 1910. Shanghaiing Charged, Two Boys Allege Ill Treatment on Lake Freighter.

Websites

Historical Collection of the Great Lakes, Bowling Green State University Library, Bowling Green, OH.

Marquette & Bessemer No.1. Historical Collection of the Great Lakes, vessels, date retrieved, 8/15/22.

Steinbrenner, Henry, Historical Collections of the Great Lakes, vessels date retrieved 7/23/2022.

Richardson, W.C., Historical Collection of the Great Lakes, vessels, date retrieved 7/30/22.

Marquette & Bessemer No. 2, Historical Collection of the Great Lakes, vessels, Date retrieved 7/25/22,

Dowsett, Kathy, August 31st, A Look Back: SS Bannockburn, AKA, "The Flying Dutchman." The Scuba News. thescubanews.com/2021/08.

Historical Collection of the Great Lakes, vessels, Lake Fresco, Bowling Green State University, Bowling Green, OH, Date retrieved 8/2/22.

U-boat.net, ships hit by U-boats/Jack. Uboat.net/allies/merchants/ship/1709.html.

August 13,th 2021, MasterMario, Vanishing Shipwreck: Lost Ships of the Great Lakes. Opposite-lock.com/topic/21603/vanishing-shipwreck-lost-ships-of-the-great-lakes.

Interviews

Sinking of the Bessemer-Local History with George Thorman, Guest Frank Prothero, Elgin County Archives, http:/www.elgincounty.ca/archives, undated.

Works Cited

i   November 3,rd 1986, Marquette & Bessemer Story Set Straight, *Ashtabula Star Beacon*, Ashtabula, OH.

ii   December 13,th 1909, Bodies of Nine Brought in From Wreck of the Carferry, *The Cleveland Plain Dealer*, Cleveland, OH. p. 1.

iii   December 11,th 1909, Fifty-Nine Lives Lost in the Storm on Lake Erie. *Duluth Evening Herald*, Duluth, MN.

iv   March 12,th 1910, Wooden Vessels Rapidly Vanishing in the Great Lakes, *The Toledo Blade*,Toledo, OH.

v   Babbish, Byron (2017), Erie, Ontario, and All the Others, Carferries of the Great Lakes, Create Space, an Amazon Company, p. 1.

vi   Hilton, George W. (1962), The Great Lakes Carferries, Howell-North Books, Berkeley, California, p. 210.

vii   Marquette & Bessemer No. 1. Historical Collection of the Great Lakes, vessels, Bowling Green State University Library,Bowling Green, OH. Date retrieved, 8/15/22.

viii Hilton, George W. (1962), The Great Lakes Carferries, Howell-North Books, Berkeley California, p. 211.

ix   February 12,th 1910, Over 65,000 Trains Would be Needed to Transport Freight Handled in Duluth Superior Harbor in 1909, *Duluth Evening Herald*, Duluth MN.

x   December 15,th 1909, Ore Shipments for the Year Beat All Former Records, *Conneaut News-Herald*, Conneaut, OH, p. 2.

xi   December 19,th1909,30 Boats Total Loss This Year., *Detroit Free Press.*

xii   *Henry Steinbrenner*, Historical Collections of the Great Lakes, vessels. Bowling Green State University Library, Bowling Green, OH. Date retrieved 7/23/2022.

xiii January 13,th 1910, *Wissahickon* is Released, *Duluth Evening Herald*, Duluth, MN.

xiv December 11,th 1909, Fifty-Nine Lives Lost in the Storm on Lake Erie, *Duluth Evening Herald*, Duluth, MN.

xv   December 11,th 1909, Fifty-Nine Lives Lost in the Storm on Lake Erie, *Duluth Evening Herald*, Duluth, MN.

xvi December 18,th 1909, Swimmer Frozen in a Cake of Ice, *Detroit Free Press*, Detroit MI.

xvii   December 11,[th] 1909, Fifty-Nine Lives Lost in the Storm on Lake Erie. *Duluth Evening Herald.*

xviii   Boyer, Dwight, (1968), Ghost Ships of the Great Lakes, NY, Dodd-Mead, p. 154.

xix   *W.C. Richardson*, Historical Collection of the Great Lakes, vessels, Bowling Green State University Library, Bowling Green, OH. Date retrieved 7/30/22.

xx   December 11,[th] 1909, Paine Towed into Port, *Cleveland Plain Dealer.*

xxi   December 13,[th] 1909. Would Cut the Season, *Duluth Evening Herald.*

xxii   February 4,[th] 1910. Incompetents Caused Loss of Richardson, *The Duluth Labor World.*

xxiii   Daley, Matthew Lawrence (Spring, 2018). An Unequal Clash: The Lake Seamen's Union, The Lake Carrier's Association, and the Great Lakes Strike of 1909. The Northern Mariner, XVIII, No. 2, p. 126.

xxiv   Daley, Matthew Lawrence (Spring, 2018). An Unequal Clash: The Lake Seamen's Union, The Lake Carrier's Association, and the Great Lakes Strike of 1909. The Northern Mariner, XVIII, No. 2, p.125.

xxv   Daley, Matthew Lawrence (Spring,2018). An Unequal Clash: The Lake Seamen's Union, The Lake Carrier's Association and the Great Lakes Strike of 1909. The Northern Mariner, XVIII, No. 2, pp. 136-137.

xxvi   Daley, Matthew Lawrence (Spring, 2018), An Unequal Clash: The Seamen's Union, The Lake Carrier's Association, and the Great Lakes Strike of 1909. The Northern Mariner, XVIII, p. 132.

xxvii Daley, Matthew Lawrence (Spring,2018). An Unequal Clash: The Lake Seamen's Union, The Lake Carrier's Association and the Great Lakes Strike of 1909. The Northern Mariner, XVIII, No. 2 p. 137.

xxviii February 5,[th] 1910, Incompetence Caused Loss of Richardson, *The Duluth Labor World.*

xxix   March 12,[th] 1910. Shanghaiing Charged, Two Boys Allege Ill Treatment on Lake Freighter. *The Toledo Blade.*

xxx   January 19,[th] 1910. Talks of Raising Premiums, *Duluth Evening Herald.*

xxxi   December 13,[th] 1909, *Erie Times News.*

xxxii   Hibbert, Andrew, November 13,[th] 2009, Part 1: Where is the
         No. 2, November 13,[th] Lake Erie Beacon, p. 3.

xxxii   December 13,[th] 1909, Fifty Float in Lake, *Grand Rapids Press*. p. 1.

xxxiii   Boyer, Dwight, (1968), Ghost Ships of the Great Lakes,
         NY, Dodd-Mead, p. 152.

xxxiv   Babbish, Byron, (2017), Erie, Ontario, and All the Others,
         Carferries of the Great Lakes, Create Space, An Amazon
         Company, p. 1.

xxxv   Babbish, Byron, (2017), Erie, Ontario, and All the Others,
         Carferries of the Great Lakes, Create Space, An Amazon
         Company, p. 5.

xxxvi   Hilton, George W. (1962), The Great Lakes Carferries, Howell-
         North Books, Berkeley, CA.

xxxvii   Byron Babbish, (2017), Erie, Ontario, and All the Others,
         Carferries of the Great Lakes, Create Apace, An Amazon
         Company, p. 5.

xxxviii *Marquette & Bessemer No. 2*, Historical Collection of the
         Great Lakes, vessels, Bowling Green State University Library,
         Date retrieved 7/25/22.

xxxix   Babbish, Byron (2017), Erie, Ontario, and All the Others,
         Carferries of the Great Lakes, Create Space, an Amazon
         Company, p. 12.

xl   Hilton, George W. (1962), The Great Lakes Carferries, Howell-
         North Books, Berkley, CA, p, 210.

xli   Hilton, George W (1962), The Great Lakes Carferries, Howell-
         North Books, Berkely CA, pp. 210-211.

xlii   December 21,[st] 1909. Car Ferries to be Equipped with
         Wireless, *Erie-Times News*, p. 1.

xliii   Babbish, Byron (2017), Erie, Ontario, and All the Others,
         Carferries of the Great Lakes, Create Space, an Amazon
         Company, p. 32.

xliv   Hilton, George W. (1962), The Great Lakes Carferries, Howell-
         North Books, Berkley CA, forward, p. 7.

xlv   Boyer, Dwight (1968),Ghost Ships of the Great Lakes, NY.
         Dodd-Mead, p. 160.

xlvi   Boyer, Dwight (1968),Ghost Ships of the Great Lakes, NY.
         Dodd-Mead, p. 160.

xlvii   Boyer, Dwight (1968),Ghost Ships of the Great Lakes, NY.
         Dodd-Mead, p.160.

xlix   Boyer, Dwight (1968), Ghost Ships of the Great Lakes. NY. Dodd-Mead, p. 94.

l   Boyer, Dwight (1968),Ghost Ships of the Great Lakes, NY. Dodd-Mead, p. 91.

li   December 13,[th] 1909. Ex-Wheelsman Tells How Cars Broke Loose Once. *The Evening Free Press*, London, ON.

lii   Unknown, undated newspaper article. Historical Collection of the Great Lakes, Bowling Green State University, Bowling Green, OH. Date retrieved, 8/20/22.

liii   December 13,[th] 1909. He did not Feel Secure, *St. Thomas Daily Times*, St. Thomas, ON.

liv   Boyer Dwight (1968), Ghost Ships of the Great Lakes, NY, NY. Dodd-Mead p. 168.

lv   December 13,[th] 1909, or there abouts. Declares Bessemer "Ghastly Mantrap," This article is probably from *The Evening Free Press* in London, ON, but this cannot be definitely confirmed. Article can be found in Marquette & Bessemer, folder 2, at the Historical Collection of the Great Lakes, Bowling Green State University, Bowling Green, OH.

lvi   Undated article, probably from *The Evening Free Press*, but cannot confirm. Historical Collection of the Great Lakes, Marquette & Bessemer No. 2, folder 2. Bowling Green State University. Bowling Green, OH.

lvii   December 13,[th] 1909. Did not Feel Secure, *St Thomas Daily Times*, St. Thomas, ON, p. 1.

lviii   December 14,[th] 1909. Couldn't Ship Enough Water, *St. Thomas Daily Times*, St. Thomas, ON.

lix   December 13,[th] 1909. Ex-Wheelsman Tells How Cars Broke Loose Once. *The Evening Free Press*, London, ON.

lx   December 11,[th] 1909, Crew of the Marquette & Bessemer No. 2 Carferry, *Conneaut News-Herald*,Conneaut, OH. p. 1.

lxi   December 10,[th] 1909. John King, A Londoner on Missing Bessemer Joined Boat Recently, *The Evening Free Press*, London ON.

lxii   December 15,[th] *Erie Times-News*, Erie, PA.

lxiii   December 15,[th] 1909. *Erie-Times News*, Erie, PA, p. 12.

lxiv   December 10,[th]1909. Capt. M'Leod has great reputation, *The Evening Free Press*, London, ON.

lxv   December 13,[th] 1909, McLeod Controlled His Boat as A Women

Manages a Go-Cart. *The Evening Free Press*, London ON, p. 1.

lxvi   December 13,[th] 1909. Ex-Wheelsman Tells How Cars Broke Loose Once. *The Evening Free Press*, London, ON.

lxvii   Historical Collection of the Great Lakes, Marquette & Bessemer No. 2, folder 2, Bowling Green State University, Bowling Green, OH.

lxviii   December 15,[th] 1909, *Erie-Times News*, Erie, PA.

lxix   Boyer, Dwight, (1968), Ghost Ships of the Great Lakes, NY, NY, Dodd-Mead, pp. 145-146.

lxx   Historical Collection of the Great Lakes, Marquette & Bessemer. folder 2, Bowling Green State University, Bowling Green, OH.

lxxi   December 15,[th] 1909, *Erie-Times News*, Erie, PA.

lxxii   Boyer, Dwight(1968), Ghost Ships of the Great Lakes. NY, Dodd-Mead, p.147.

lxxiii   Historical Collection of the Great Lakes, Marquette & Bessemer No. 2, folder 2. Bowling Green State University, Bowling Green, OH.

lxxiv   December 15,[th] 1909, *Erie-Times News*, Erie PA.

lxxv   Boyer, Dwight, (1968), Ghost Ships of the Great Lakes. NY, Dodd-Mead, p. 146.

lxxvi   December 15,[th] 1909, *Erie-Times News*, Erie PA.

lxxvii   December 15,[th] 1909, *Erie-Times News*, Erie PA.

lxxviii   December 15,[th] 1909, *Erie-Times News*, Erie, PA.

lxxix   Historical Collection of the Great Lakes, Marquette & Bessemer No. 2. folder 2, Bowling Green State University, Bowling Green, OH.

lxxx   December 15,[th] 1909, *Erie-Times News*, Erie PA.

lxxxi   Historical Collection of the Great Lakes, Marquette & Bessemer No. 2 folder 2, Bowling Green State University, Bowling Green, OH.

lxxxii   December 15,[th] 1909, *Erie-Times News*, Erie, PA.

lxxxiii   December 15,[th] 1909, *Erie-Times News*, Erie, PA.

lxxxiv   December 15,[th] 1909, *Erie Times-News*, Erie, PA.

lxxv   December 18,[th] 1909, Only Support of Parents in Scotland was Charles Crutts, Carferry Victim. Pg.1, *Conneaut News-Herald*, Conneaut, OH.

lxxvi   December 15th, 1909, *Erie Times-News*, Erie, PA.

lxxxvii   Boyer, Dwight (1968), Ghost Ships of the Great Lakes. NY. Dodd-Mead, p. 149.

lxxxviii   Historical Collection of the Great Lakes, Marquette & Bessemer No. 2 folder 2, Bowling Green State University, Bowling Green, OH.
December 15th, 1909, *Erie Times News*, Erie PA, p. 12.

lxxxix   Historical Collection of the Great Lakes, Marquette & Bessemer No.2 folder 2, Bowling Green State University, Bowling Green,OH.

xc   Historical Collection of the Great Lakes, Marquette & Bessemer No. 2 Folder 2, Bowling Green State University, Bowling Green, OH.

xci   December 15,[th] 1909, *Erie Times-News*, Erie, PA, p. 12.

xcii   Historical Collection of the Great Lakes, Marquette & Bessemer No. 2 Folder 2, Bowling Green State University, Bowling Green, OH.

xciii   December 11,[th] 1909, Crew of the Marquette & Bessemer No.2 Carferry, *Conneaut News-Herald*, Conneaut, OH, p. 1.

xciv   Historical Collection of the Great Lakes, Marquette & Bessemer No. 2, Folder 2. Bowling Green State University, Bowling Green, OH.

xcv   Historical Collection of the Great Lakes, Marquette & Bessemer No. 2 Folder 2, Bowling Green State University, Bowling Green, OH.

xcvi   December 14,[th] 1909, Ill Fated Car Ferry Close to Harbor Vessel Whose Crew of 32 Men Perished, *Cleveland Plain Dealer*, Cleveland, OH, p. 9.

xcvii   December 16,[th] 1909, O'Hagan Not on Ferry, The *Erie Times-News*, Erie PA, p. 5.

xcviii   Historical Collection of the Great Lakes. This article is in the Marquette & Bessemer No. 2. Folder 2. There is a high probability that it is from the December 13th, 1909 *London Evening Free Press*, London ON, but this cannot be absolutely confirmed.

xcix   December 13,[th] 1909, One of Bessemer's Victims New Sarum Lad, St. Thomas Daily Times, St. Thomas, ON.

c   December 16,[th] 1909, Many Lives Lost on Lake Erie, The *Simcoe Reformer*, Simcoe ON, p. 1.

ci   December 17th, 1909, Carferry Continues to be Topic of Interest-Letters and Rumors, *Conneaut News-Herald*,

cii   December 17th, 1909, Carferry Continues to be Topic of Interest-Letters and Rumors, *Conneaut News-Herald*, Conneaut, OH. p.1.

ciii   December 13,[th] 1909, *St Thomas Daily Times*, St. Thomas, OH. p. 1.

civ   Historical Collection of the Great Lakes, Marquette & Bessemer No. 2. Folder 2, Bowling Green State University, Bowling Green, OH.

cv   December 13,[th] 1909, Boat Containing Nine Frozen Bodies Tells the Fate of the Bessemer, *The Evening Free Press*, London ON.

cvi   Boyer, Dwight, (1968) Ghost Ships of the Great Lakes. NY. Dodd-Mead, p. 148.

cvii   December 17,[th] 1909, *Flint Journal*, Flint, MI.

cviii   December 18,[th] 1909, Probably the *London Evening Free Press*, but cannot confirm. Historical Collection of the Great Lakes, Marquette & Bessemer No. 2, Folder 2, Bowling Green State University, Bowling Green, OH.

cix   December 18,[th] 1909, Wirtz Taking Last Trip, *Flint Journal*, Flint MI, p. 8.

cx   December 13,[th] Associated Press Dispatch, Historical Collection of the Great Lakes, Marquette & Bessemer No. 2, folder 2, Bowling Green State University, Bowling Green, OH.

cxi   Historical Collection of the Great Lakes, Marquette & Bessemer No. 2, Folder 2, Bowling Green State University, Bowling Green, OH.

cxii   December 11,[th] 1909, Erie Man on the Carferry, *Erie Times-News*, Erie PA, p. 16.

cxiii   December 13,[th] 1909, *Erie Times-News*, Erie, PA, p. 2.

cxiv   December 13,[th] 1909, Bodies of Nine Brought in From the Wreck of the Carferry Lost in Great Strom, *Cleveland Plain Dealer*, Cleveland OH, p. 2.

cxv   December 11,[th]1909, Painful Accident was Lucky for Michael. *St. Thomas Daily Times*, St. Thomas ON, p.1.

cxvi   December 16,[th] 1909, Will Take Another Chance, *Erie Times-News*, Erie, PA, p. 3.

cxvii   Undated, London Man Missed the Boat on Monday Being Late Saved His Life. Unknown newspaper, probably the *London Free Press*. Marquette & Bessemer No. 2 Folder 2, Bowling Green State University, Bowling Green, OH.

cxviii December 13,[th] 1909, Three Members of the Crew are Safe, *The Evening Free Press*, London, ON.

cxix   December 11,th 1909, *The St. Thomas Journal*, St. Thomas, ON.

cxx   Boyer, Dwight, (1968) Ghost Ships of the Great Lakes, NY, NY, Dodd-Mead, pg. 152.

cxxi   December 11th, 1909, Fifty-Nine Lives lost in Storm on the Lake Erie, *Duluth Evening Herald*, pg. 1.

cxxii   December 14,th 1909, Seas Ran Too High, *St. Thomas Daily Times*, pg. 1, St. Thomas, ON.

cxxiii   December 9,th 1909, Conditions Blizzard are More Severe Than Anticipated, *Conneaut News-Herald*, Conneaut, OH.

cxxiv   December 13,th 1909, Lake Pilot Says Bessemer Sunk if She Attempted to Turn Around. *The Evening Free Press*, London, ON, pg. 1.

cxxv   Boyer, Dwight, (1968), Ghost Ships of the Great Lakes, NY, NY, Dodd-Mead, p. 156.

cxxvi   Boyer, Dwight, (1968), Ghost Ships of the Great Lakes. NY, Dodd-Mead, p. 162.

cxxvii   December 15,th Did the Car Ferry Turn Back to Conneaut Harbor. *Erie Times News*, Erie, PA, p. 12.

cxxviii   December 13,th 1909, Believed Car Ferry Was Off Local Harbor and Close in Wednesday Morning. *Conneaut News-Herald*, Conneaut, OH p. 1.

cxxix   December 14,th 1909. Car Ferry Not Near Harbor, *Conneaut New Herald, Conneaut, OH*.

cxxx   December 8,th 1909, Delayed by Low Water, *Cleveland Plain Dealer*, Cleveland, OH.

cxxxi   December 8,th 1909, Marine News, *Cleveland Plain Dealer*, Cleveland OH.

cxxxii   December 8,th 1909, Marine News, *Cleveland Plain Dealer*, Cleveland OH.

cxxxiii   December 8,th 1909, Marine News, *Cleveland Plain Dealer*, Cleveland, OH.

cxxxiv   December 13,th 1909, Car Ferry Was Off the Local Harbor and Close in Wednesday Morning, *Conneaut News Herald*, Conneaut, OH, p. 1.

cxxxv   Boyer, Dwight, (1968), Ghost Ships of the Great Lakes, Dodd-Mead. NY, p. 154.

cxxxvi   December 13,th 1909, PM Carferry No. 19 Will Take Place Bessemer's Place on Lake Run, *The Evening Free Press*, London ON.

cxxxvii December 16,[th] 1909. Saw Car Ferry Near Shore, *Erie Times News*, Erie PA, p. 3.

cxxxviii Boyer, Dwight, (1968), Ghost Ships of the Great Lakes, Dodd-Mead, NY, pp. 155-156.

cxxxix Boyer, Dwight, (1968), Ghost Ships of the Great Lakes, Dodd-Mead, NY. p. 156.

cxxxl   Boyer, Dwight, (1968), Ghost Ships of the Great Lakes, Dodd-Mead, NY, p. 157.

cxli   December 13,[th] 1909, Ferry Went Down But A Few Miles Out, *The Evening Free Press*, London, ON, p. 1.

cxlii   December 13,[th] 1909, Heard Distress Whistles, *St. Thomas Daily Times*, St. Thomas, ON.

cxliii December 16,[th] Minister of Marine Orders Probe of Bessemer Wreck, *The Evening Free Press*, London ON.

cxliv   Historical Collection of the Great Lakes, Marquette & Bessemer No. 2, Folder 2. Bowling Green State University, Bowling Green, OH.

cxlv   May 15,[th] 1910, The Ugly Secret Tucked Away in a Little Inland Sea, *Cleveland Plain Dealer*, Cleveland OH, p. 60.

cxlvi   December 14,[th] 1909, This Story Says the Carferry Still Afloat Early Thursday Morning, *Conneaut News-Herald*, Conneaut, OH, pg 1.

cxlvii Hibbert, Andrew, November 13th, 2009, where is the No. 2? The Lake Erie Beacon, pp. 3-5.

cxlviii December 17,[th] 1909, In Waking Vision Saw Bessemer Sink, *The Evening Free Press*, London, ON.

cxlix   Boyer, Dwight, (1968) Ghost Ships of the Great Lakes, Dodd-Mead, NY, p. 157.

cl   December 14,[th] 1909, No. 1 did not search for the No. 2, *Conneaut News-Herald*, Conneaut, OH, p. 1.

cli   Historical Collection of the Great Lakes, Marquette & Bessemer No. 2 Folder No. 2, Bowling Green State University, Bowling Green, OH.

clii   December 13,[th] 1909, Body of Roy Hinds among those brought into Port on Monday, *The Evening Free Press*, London, ON.

cliii   December 13,[th] 1909, Bodies of Nine Brought in From Wreck of Car Ferry Lost in Great Storm, *The Cleveland Plain Dealer*, Cleveland OH, p. 2.

cliv   December 13,[th] 1909, Nine Frozen Bodies Found, One Was Port Stanley Boy, *St. Thomas Daily Times*, St. Thomas, ON, p. 1.

clv   December 13,[th] 1909, Carferry Foundered Weds. A.M., Nine
        Bodies Recovered Yesterday, *Conneaut New-Herald*,
        Conneaut, OH, p. 1

clvi   December 13,[th] 1909, Bodies of Nine Brought In From the
        Wreck of The Car Ferry Lost in the Great Storm. *Cleveland
        Plain Dealer*, Cleveland OH, p. 2.

clvii   December 13,[th] 1909, Nine Storm Victims Found Floating in
        Icy Yawl Boat, *Erie Times-News*, Erie, Pa, p. 1.

clviii December 13,[th] 1909, The *Cleveland Plain Dealer*, Cleveland,
        OH.

clix   Boyer, Dwight (1968), Ghost Ships of the Great Lakes, Dodd-
        Mead, NY. p. 156.

clx   December 13,[th] 1909, Nine Frozen Bodies Found, One Was
        PT. Stanley Boy, *The Saint Thomas Daily Times*, St. Thomas,
        ON.

clxi   Boyer, Dwight (1968), Ghost Ships of the Great Lakes,
        Dodd-Mead, NY, p. 164.

clxii   Boyer, Dwight (1968), Ghost Ships of the Great Lakes,
        Dodd-Mead, NY, p. 159.

clxiii December 13,[th] 1909. Car Ferry Foundered Wed. A.M., Nine
        Bodies Recovered Yesterday. *Conneaut News Herald*,
        Conneaut, OH. p. 1.

clxiv   December 13,[th] 1909, McLeod Controlled His Boat as a
        Women Manages a Go-Cart, *The Evening Free Press*, London,
        ON, p. 1.

clxv   December 11,[th] Farmers Find Bessemer Boat and Wreckage,
        The Evening Free Press, London, ON.

clxvi   December 11,[th] 1909, Bodies of Three Men Washed Ashore at
        Clear Creek, *St. Thomas Daily Times*, St. Thomas, ON, p. 1.

clxvii December 13,[th] About Finding Three Bodies, Yawl Boat Not
        Seen by Port Burrell Boat Winner, *St Thomas Daily Times*, St.
        Thomas, ON.

clxviii December 13,[th] Port Stanley Citizens Report to Have Heard the
        Whistle of the Bessemer, *St. Thomas Daily Times*, St Thomas,
        ON.

clxix   Boyer, Dwight, (1968), Ghost Ships of the Great Lakes, Dodd-
        Mead, NY, p. 165.

clxx   December 14,[th] 1909, Another Lifeboat is Found, *St Thomas
        Daily Times*, St. Thomas, ON, p. 1.

clxxi Boyer, Dwight, (1968), Ghost Ships of the Great Lakes, Dodd-Mead, NY, p. 165.

clxxii December 15,[th] 1909, Another Yawl Boat is Found on the Canadian Side, *Conneaut News-Herald*, Conneaut, OH, p. 1.

clxxiii December 11,[th] 1909, *The Cleveland Plain Dealer*, Cleveland OH, p. 1.

clxxiv August 9,[th] 1964, Couple May Solve 1909 Ship Mystery, *Cleveland Plain Dealer*, Cleveland OH,

clxxv December 13,[th] 1909, Curled Up in the Bottom of the Boat, *Erie-Times News*, Erie, PA. p. 1.

clxxvi December 13,[th] Fifty Float in Lake, *Grand Rapids Press*, Grand Rapids, MI, p. 5.

clxxvii December 14,[th] 1909, Council Adjourned Out of Respect for the Crew of the Carferry, *Conneaut News-Herald*, Conneaut, OH.

clxxviii Historical Collection of the Great Lakes, Bowling Green State University, Bowling Green, OH., 08/31/22

clxxix Historical Collection of the Great Lakes, Bowling Green State University, Bowling Green OH. Retrieved 07/22/22.

clxxx December 14,[th] 1909, *Butler Citizen*, Butler PA, p. 8.

clxxxi Historical Collection of the Great Lakes, Bowling Green State University, Bowling Green, OH. Retrieved 07/22/22.

clxxxii Historical Collection of the Great Lakes, Bowling Green State University, Bowling Green, OH, Retrieved on 07/22/22.

clxxxiii Historical Collection of the Great Lakes, Bowling Green State University, Bowling Green, OH.

clxxiv Boyer, Dwight, (1968), Ghost Ships of the Great Lakes, Dodd-Mead, NY. p 164.

clxxxv May 2,[th] 1910, *The Buffalo Evening News*, Buffalo NY.

clxxxvi April 10,[th] 1910, Chief Engineer Wood's Body Found in Lake Near Pt. Colborne Today, *Conneaut News Herald*, Conneaut OH, p 1.

clxxxvii Historical Collection of the Great Lakes, Bowling Green State University, Bowling Green OH, Retrieved 07/22/22.

clxxxviii October 11,[th] 1910, Another Body Found, *Cleveland Plain Dealer*, Cleveland, OH, p. 13.

clxxxix Boyer, Dwight, (1968), Ghost Ships of the Great Lakes, Dodd-Mead, NY, p. 167.

cxc April 7,[th] 1910, Body of Bessemer Captain is Found, *The Evening Free Press*, London ON, p. 1.

cxci April 7,[th] 1910, *Buffalo Evening News*, Buffalo, NY.

cxcii Historical Collection of the Great Lakes, Bowling Green State University, Bowling Green, OH

cxciii April 30,[th] 1910, Find Another Victim, *The Erie Times News*, Erie, PA. p. 9.

cxciv July 26,[th] 1910, Floater May be Victim of the Ferry Wreck. *The Erie-Times News*, Erie PA, p. 1.

cxcv September 21,[st] 1910, *Cleveland Plain Dealer*, Cleveland, OH, p. 6.

cxcvi October 2,[nd] 1910, *Cleveland Plain Dealer*, Cleveland, OH.

cxcvii October 7,[th] 1910, Body of Captain M'Leod of Carferry Found. *Erie Times-News*, Erie, PA, p. 6.

cxcviii October 7,[th] 1910, Capt. McLeod's Body Found, *The Cleveland Plain Dealer*, Cleveland, OH, p. 11.

cxcix Boyer, Dwight, (1968), Ghost Ships of the Great Lakes, Dodd-Mead, NY, NY, p. 165.

cc October 3,[rd] 1910, Body Found Not That of Albert Weis, *Erie Times-Times News*, Erie, PA, p. 6.

cci December 10,[th] 1909, Car Ferry Conneaut Probably Gone Down. *Erie-Times News*.

ccii December 11,[th] 1909, *Cleveland Plain Dealer*.

cciii Hibbert, Andrew, November 13,[th] 2009, Part 1: Where is the No. 2? The Lake Erie Beacon, pp. 3-6.

cciv December 9,[th] 1909, Marine News, *Cleveland Plain Dealer*, Cleveland, OH.

ccv December 17,[th] 1909, Missing Car Ferry Located, *Erie Times-News*, Erie PA, p. 6.

ccvi December 18,[th] 1909, Car Ferry Wreck Found Near Erie, *Duluth News-Tribune*, Duluth MN, p. 10.

ccvii December 17,[th] 1909, Associated Press Dispatch, No Wreckage of the Bessemer II Found. Newspaper unknown, Marquette & Bessemer No. 2, Folder 2. Historical Collection of the Great Lakes, Bowling Green State University, Bowling Green OH, retrieved August 10th, 2022.

ccviii April 1,[st] 1910, Carferry Wreckage is Found by Boys, *Erie-Times News*, Erie, PA, p. 4.

ccix September 1,[st] 1910, Finds Carferry Wreck? *Cleveland Plain Dealer*, Cleveland OH, pg 3.

ccx March 15,[th] 1910, Divers May Search for the Lost Carferry, *Erie Times-News*, Erie, PA, p. 5.

ccxi   March 11,th 1910, Wreck of the Ill-Fated Car Ferry Found, *Erie Times-News*, Erie, PA, p. 12.

ccxii   March 12,th 1910, Lost Car Ferry May be Off Port Bruce, *Buffalo Evening News*, Buffalo, NY.

ccxiii   May 17,th 1910, May Search for the Bessemer, *Detroit Free Press*, Detroit, MI.

ccxiv   October 8th, 1910, Believe Carferry sunk of this city. *Erie Times-News*, Erie PA, p. 2

ccxv   April 23,th 1914, Practical Joker Wrote Message, *Erie Times-News*, Erie, PA, p. 3.

ccxvi   May 17,th 1928, Clew to The Fate of the Bessemer, *Conneaut New-Herald*, Conneaut, OH, p. 1.

ccxvii   July 21,st 1932, Notice to Mariners, *Cleveland Plain Dealer*, Cleveland, OH, p. 10.

ccxviii   July 24,th 1932, Hear Carferry Sunk in 1909 is Located, *Cleveland Plain Dealer*, Cleveland, OH, p. 17.

ccxix   Historical Collection of the Great Lakes, vessels, Bowling Green State University, Bowling Green, OH. Date retrieved 8/2/22.

ccxx   U-boat.net, ships hit by U-boats/Jack. Uboat.net/allies/merchants/ship/1709.html.

ccxxi   Boyer, Dwight, (1968), Ghost Ships of the Great Lakes, Dodd-Mead, NY, NY, p. 170.

ccxxii   August 9,th 1964, Couple May Solve 1909 Ship Mystery, *Cleveland Plain Dealer*, Cleveland, OH.

ccxxiii   November 26,th 1989, Lake Erie's Wrath Felt 80 Years Ago, *The News-Herald*, Conneaut, OH.

ccxxiv   May 1,st 1975, Wreck Believed Found, *London Free Press*, London, ON.

ccxxv   Historical Collection of the Great Lakes, Marquette & Bessemer No. 2, Folder 2. Bowling Green State University, Bowling Green, OH.

ccxxvi   Sinking of the Bessemer-Local History with George Thorman, Guest Frank Prothero, Elgin County Archives, http:/www.elgincounty.ca/archives, undated.

ccxxvii   Boyer, Dwight, (1968), Ghost Ships of the Great Lakes, Dodd-Mead, NY, p. 157.

ccxxviii   December 16,th 1909, No. 1 did not search for the No. 2. *The Conneaut News-Herald*, Conneaut OH, p. 1.

ccxxix Hibbert, Andrew, November 13,[th] 2009. Part 1: Where is the No. 2? Lake Erie Beacon, pp. 3-5.

ccxxx   December 13,[th] Heard Distress Whistles, Probable Port Stanley newspaper, unable to confirm. Marquette & Bessemer No. 2, folder 2. Historical Collection of the Great Lakes, Bowling Green State University, Bowling Green, OH.

ccxxxi Boyer, Dwight, (1968), Ghost Ships of the Great Lakes, Dodd-Mead, NY, p. 168.

ccxxxii March 15,[th] 1910, Divers May Search for the Lost Ferry, *Erie Times-News*, Erie, PA, p. 5.

ccxxxiii December 15,[th] 1909, The Season on The Lakes, *The Duluth Evening Herald*, Duluth, MN.

ccxxxiv News Editor, The Mystery of the C.B. Lockwood, https://ontariomarineheritagecommittee.ca/the-mystery-of-the-c-b-lockwood/, March 2017.

ccxxxv August 13,[th] 2021, Master Mario, Vanishing Shipwreck: Lost Ships of the Great Lakes. Opposite-lock.com/topic/21603 vanishing-shipwreck-lost-ships-of-the-great-lakes

www.ingramcontent.com/pod-product-compliance
Lightning Source LLC
Chambersburg PA
CBHW050828180425
25257CB00001B/1